US ARMY
HANDBOOK
1939–1945

'Old Glory' is raised once again on Corregidor, three years after the Japanese tore it down, while paratroopers of 503rd Para Inf Regt salute. Gen MacArthur (arrowed) said: 'Hoist the Stars and Stripes and let no enemy ever haul them down.'

US ARMY
HANDBOOK
1939–1945

GEORGE FORTY

SUTTON PUBLISHING

This book was first published in 1979 by Ian Allan.

First published by Sutton Publishing in 1995

This edition first published in 2003 by
Sutton Publishing Limited · Phoenix Mill
Thrupp · Stroud · Gloucestershire · GL5 2BU

British Library Cataloguing in Publication Data
A catalogue record for this book is available from the British Library.

ISBN 0 7509 3210 4

Typeset in 10/13pt Sabon.
Typesetting and origination by
Sutton Publishing Limited.
Printed and bound in Great Britain by
J. H. Haynes & Co. Ltd, Sparkford.

CONTENTS

INTRODUCTION

The building of the American Army in World War II from a tiny, outdated and ill equipped force, into one of the mightiest armies in the world, was rightly described by the late Sir Winston Churchill as being a 'prodigy of organisation'. Its value to the Allied cause was immeasurable and it had a fine fighting record all over the world. It was a marvellously well equipped army, thanks to American inventiveness, 'know-how' and technical prowess. And of course America generously supplied billions and billions of dollars worth of military equipment and supplies to the other Allied nations throughout the war.

The catalogue of superlatives could go on and on, so perhaps it is a good thing that this book is written by an Englishman, or the reader might well consider that this was not an unbiased study! However, one cannot fail but be impressed by the things which were achieved and the speed in which they were all done. It is difficult not to become overawed by the sheer size of both the problems faced and the solutions found to them. As one might expect, the recording of these achievements was a monumental task in itself and the resulting history of the United States Army in World War II is a very large and detailed work, running into some 80 volumes and written by the most eminent American military historians. For me to compress all their work into this small book has meant leaving out an enormous amount of material. I have, for example, had to concentrate upon the Army Ground Forces and to virtually ignore the Army Service Forces and Army Air Forces. Even then I have had to focus upon the divisional level and below, mentioning only briefly the all important non divisional troops, which made up over half the tactical forces of the US Army. This has been inevitable, but I do hope that anyone who wants to delve more deeply will find the select bibliography of value.

It may be of interest if I explain how I, a retired British Army officer, came to write a handbook on the US Army in World War II. The simple answer is because one did not exist, so even my puny efforts are better than nothing at all. Although there are many excellent books which cover specialised segments – such as insignia, dress, weapons and vehicles, there is no compact handbook which draws them all together with organisations, tactics etc. on sale in the UK. I found this particularly frustrating when I was researching for my book *Patton's Third Army at War*, so I decided that I would write one at the earliest opportunity. I hope that the result will be of use to all wargamers, modellers and all those who, like me, find a special fascination in the 'nitty gritty' about the forces of any nation.

I would like to thank my good friend George F. Hofmann of Cincinnati, who, at very short notice, read through the manuscript of this book and made a number of most helpful and useful comments. He has also let me quote from his history of the 6th Armoured Division *The Super Sixth* for which I am very grateful.

I have many other people to thank for their invaluable help in the preparation of this book, in particular the Ministry of Defence Library and the Royal United Services Library who have lent me many books for long periods. Also the Imperial War Museum, both the Department of Photographs and of Printed Books, who have been their usual charming and helpful selves, the Tank Museum at Bovington Camp and the following agencies and individuals: Capt Charles L. Blische and the staff of the US Army Audio-Visual Activity; Lt-Gen Sir Napier Crookenden; John S. Duvall, chief curator of the 82nd Airborne Division Historical Society; Col James H. Leach of Arlington, Virginia; Lt-Col Frederick E. Oldinsky of San Antonio, Texas; Master Sgt Peters of 82nd Airborne Museum, Fort Bragg; Norman L. Phillips of Poway, California; Charles A. Shaughnessy of the Modern Military Branch of the Military Archives Division, US National Archives and Record Service; John L. Slonaker, Chief of the Historical Reference Section of the US Army Military History Institute; Col William F. Strobridge, Chief of the Historical Reference Services Division of the US Center of Military History; Lt-Gen Volney F. Warner, CG HQ XVIII Airborne Corps, US Army.

INTRODUCTION TO THIS NEW EDITION

This was the first of the three Army Handbooks I have written and it was originally produced in pocketsize. However, I am delighted that Sutton Publishing has now decided to upgrade its dimensions so as to bring it in line with the others (*British Army Handbook* and *Japanese Army Handbook*). The expansion of the US Army during the Second World War into one of the mightiest armies that the world has ever known, was an incredible undertaking and certainly one deserving a larger volume. So my thanks go to all at Sutton Publishing for their hard work in producing it in this new format.

George Forty
Bryantspuddle
May 2003

GLOSSARY

AA	Anti-aircraft
A/B	Airborne
AM&S	Admin Mess & Supply
Armd	Armored
Arty	Artillery
ATk	Anti-tank
Bde	Brigade
Bn	Battalion
Cav	Cavalry
Comm	Communications
ComZ	Communications Zone
Coy	Company
CZ	Combat Zone
Div	Division
Engr	Engineer
ETO	European Theatre of Operations
Fd	Field
GMC	Gun motor carriage
Gp	Group
How	Howitzer
Hy	Heavy
Inf	Infantry
Lt	Light
Maint	Maintenance
Mech	Mechanised
Med	Medical
Med	Medium
(H/L/S)MG	(Heavy/Light/Sub-) Machine Gun
MP	Military Police
Offr	Officer
Ord	Ordnance
Pl	Platoon
QM	Quartermaster
Recce	Reconnaissance
Sect	Section
SP	Self-propelled
Sqn	Squadron
Tptn	Transportation
Tp	Troop

HISTORICAL BACKGROUND

'A PRODIGY OF ORGANISATION'

By the end of World War II the United States Army was perhaps the mightiest in the world, numbering 8,300,000 out of a total of 12,350,000 of the American Armed Forces. It was only exceeded in manpower by the Russians, and it led the world in weaponry (apart from numbers of tanks), strategic mobility and logistic capabilities. Winston Churchill described this 'prodigy of organisation' as: 'an achievement which soldiers of every other country will always study with admiration and envy.' When one compares this situation with the woefully inadequate state of the American Army in 1939, when it could best be described as that of a third rate military power, most of whose units were still trained to the combat styles of 1918 (with certain exceptions like Col Chaffee's 7th Cavalry Brigade), rather than those needed to meet the oncoming blitzkrieg which the Germans were poised to unleash, then the magnitude of this achievement is seen in its proper perspective.

MIDSUMMER 1939

On 1 July 1939, the total strength of the active Army of the United States was approximately 174,000, three quarters of whom were scattered throughout the continental United States in over 130 posts, camps and stations. The other quarter were overseas. Corps headquarters, such as they were, functioned in an administrative rather than a tactical capacity, whilst army commands existed only in theory. Of the existing nine Infantry Divisions only the 1st, 2nd and 3rd had even a framework of a divisional organisation, the rest being merely understrength brigades. The 1st and 2nd Cavalry Divisions were each over 1,200 men short and woefully equipped. There was but one mechanised brigade (7th Cavalry) and a few other oddments. Lack of motor transport made divisional training impossible and Army training funds were less than 5 per cent of the annual War Department appropriations.

'America on the march'. The US Army on parade at the start of the war. They wear the old-style World War I steel helmets, greatcoats with webbing belts and straps over the top and carry Springfield rifles, except for the officers in the front rank who carry pistols.

The Regular Army was supported by the National Guard, which numbered about 200,000 men. The first National Guard units to be set up had been the Boston Militia of 1636. Each state had its own Guard until 1933, when the National Guard of the United States came into being. The actual state of their training was regarded with some suspicion by their regular counterparts, as they drilled for only 48 evenings a year and attended a mere two weeks' of field duty. Their equipment and weapons were in short supply and of an even more antique vintage than that of the regulars, who still had the 1903 Springfield rifle and World War I trench mortars. The National Guard had little opportunity to train with the regulars, so had to content themselves with mock exercises using make-believe stove-pipe mortars and dump trucks labelled as tanks! On the credit side, however, they did contain the partially trained cadres of 18 embryo divisions.

The third element of the Army was known as the Organised Reserves. Although this existed only in the mobilisation blueprints, it did contain a pool of over 100,000 trained officers, mainly graduates of the Reserve Officers' Training Corps, which was to prove an invaluable asset to the country when the expansion programme began.

On 8 September 1939, President Franklin Delano Roosevelt declared a limited national emergency, which raised the strength of the Regular Army to 227,000 – it had already been allowed to increase from 174,000 to

210,000 in July 1939, but this increase had been entirely taken up in enlarging the garrison in Panama and in the Army Air Corps. The National Guard were also authorised to recruit to 235,000. Although these were small concessions, they did at least enable the General Staff to establish several tactical corps headquarters and enough army troops to create a fully functioning field Army. These steps were followed in April 1940 by the first proper corps manoeuvres to be held since 1918, and in May 1940 corps versus corps exercises took place, including the first tests of new weapons and tactics. In addition, the emergency proclamation permitted the expansion of the officer corps, by allowing the assignment of reserve officers to active duty. Some emergency expenditure was also permitted, including 12 million dollars for the purchase of much needed motor transport. Gen George C. Marshall, who had taken over the appointment of Chief of Staff on 1 September 1939 from Gen Malin Craig, ordered among other projects a basic reorganisation of the infantry division. This involved reorganising the three and a half existing incomplete four regiment 'square' divisions, into five smaller three-regiment 'triangular' divisions, affording far greater manoeuvrability and flexibility. Once the new organisation had been fully tested on the 1940 spring manoeuvres, all divisions, including those of the National Guard, were reorganised as triangular. Despite this boost, the US Army could, by early the following year, put only 75,000 troops into the field in a crisis, 'with only 15 of the 1,420 X 37 mm guns that had been ordered and only 140 modern 75s of the 1,430 on order' (*The Army Almanac*; The Stackpole Company).

1940 AND SELECTIVE SERVICE

During May and June 1940 the German avalanche swept across Europe. France was eliminated as a world power and Britain 'stood alone', with invasion imminent. Everywhere the swastika of the Third Reich was in the ascendancy. The gravity of the situation suddenly appeared to strike home to the people of the United States, and the threat that it posed to their security was at last recognised by everyone. This caused certain elements of the public to demand urgent and enormous increases in men and equipment for the armed forces. Large sums of money were authorised by Congress and the Selective Service Act was signed by the President on 16 September 1940. This act authorised the strength of the Army to be raised to 1,400,000 men, of which 500,000 were to be Regulars, 270,000 National Guard and 630,000 Selectees. A month later, in schools and public buildings all over the country, men between the ages of 21 and 35 started registering under the new law. Between early October 1940 and July 1941 17,000,000 men were registered, but of these only 900,000 were permitted by the Act to be inducted for service in the Army. A few weeks before Pearl Harbor, Congress renewed the Selective Service Act by a majority of only one vote in the House of Representatives.

1941 AND PEARL HARBOR

By midsummer 1941, the Army had increased eightfold and had almost reached the agreed new ceiling of 1,400,000 men. The ground forces in

Gen George C. Marshall, Chief of Staff US Army, visiting Germany in May 1945, talks with Gens Patton and Gaffey, while Gen Bradley looks on. Patton's bull terrier Willie has heard it all before! (via Patton Museum)

Secretary of War, Henry L. Stimson, during a tour of Normandy in the summer of 1944, with Gens Bradley and Patton. (via Patton Museum)

the continental United States now consisted of four armies, containing nine corps and made up of 29 divisions, plus overseas garrisons, including Alaska and Newfoundland. The picture on the equipment and weapons scene was still far from good, due in no small way to the President's policy, decided soon after the fall of France, that the USA must assist in keeping fighting Great Britain and any other effective enemies of Nazi Germany, even at the expense of American rearmament. The General Staff were most unhappy with this policy, but Gen Marshall loyally supported his commander-in-chief. Fig 1 (overleaf) shows the tactical organisation of the United States Army as at 30 June 1941.

On Sunday, 7 December 1941, the United States of America was dramatically brought into the war with the surprise attack on Pearl Harbor by the Japanese. The first bombing began at 0755 and in two hours it was all over. The US Pacific Fleet had lost 18 warships, including eight battleships sunk or damaged, 188 American aircraft had been destroyed and 3,581 sailors killed and wounded. This attack and the declaration of war by Germany and Italy which immediately followed, involved the American nation in a global conflict the like of which has never been seen before. It was to be fought in several different theatres of war, with lines of communication encircling the globe. There was now so much to do and so little time to do it in. Mobilisation had to be completed as quickly as possible, so as to develop fully the potential of the whole of the country. Men had to be

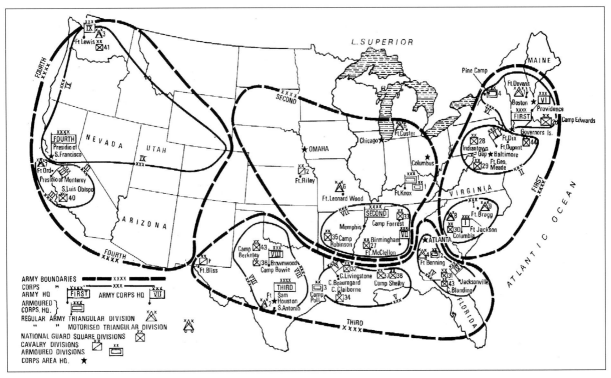

Fig 1 Tactical Organisation of the US Army as of 30 June 1941. (Source: Biennial Report of Chief of Staff US Army, 1939–41)

'I shall return!' Gen Douglas MacArthur wades ashore on Leyte Island on his return to the Philippines in 1944. President Sergio Osmena is wearing the solar topee.

inducted and trained, industrial capacity and output expanded, and all military facilities increased to unheard-of proportions.

In consequence, during this initial period of the war, the USA was purely on the defensive and, like her allies, suffered many humiliations at the hands of the Axis powers, because she was too impotent to strike back. All American effort was directed to the rapid deployment of what men and resources there were available, so as to check the momentum of the enemy assaults. At the same time protected lines of communication had to be established all around the world, while a vast expansion of naval and military establishments was begun. It took the USA in collaboration with her allies about eight months to accumulate the weapons they required, to train the men they needed *initially* and then to transport them to the various theatres of war where they could be employed in offensive action against the enemy. The end of this phase was marked by their first successful assault in August 1942 against the Japanese, at Guadalcanal and Tulagi in the Solomons.

There is neither the space nor the necessity to detail the campaigns in which the American Army and those of her allies took part during World War II, but it is true to say that in no other period of American history have the Stars and Stripes been carried so victoriously on so many battlefields. In North Africa, Sicily, Italy, North-West Europe and all over the Pacific, they took a major part in the fighting, becoming far more involved than they had ever been in World War I. The war was a climax of American military history and in areas such as amphibious warfare the USA made a unique and major contribution to the art of warfare.

C H A P T E R   2

MOBILISATION AND TRAINING

Over and under the hurdles. GIs toughen up at a Replacement Training Centre (RTC) early in the war.

In December 1941 the strength of the US Army stood at 1,686,000; 36 divisions had been activated – 29 infantry, five armoured and two cavalry. Of these divisions only two were located outside the continental United States, the remaining 34 were all short of essential items of equipment and only 17 had received sufficient training to be considered ready for combat. It was estimated that had all the critical weapons and items of equipment been pooled, then there would have been sufficient only to equip five infantry and two armoured divisions

to full scales. GHQ had estimated that an army of about 200 divisions would be needed to fight the war and an immediate target was set to raise 72 divisions by the end of 1942.

MOBILISATION

Reduced to its simplest terms, the original mobilisation and expansion plan for the field forces had the following main features:

a   Regular Army units would be brought up to scale
b   The National Guard would be inducted into Federal service and its units brought up to full strength
c   Units of the Organised Reserves would be activated
d   The training nucleus for each of these new units would be drawn from existing units
e   Enlisted and new units would be brought up to full strength by voluntary recruitment or draft, and before assignment would be put through a basic training course at replacement training centres
f   Officers for these new units would be drawn mainly from the Officers' Reserve Corps to supplement the cadre officers
g   Armies would be brought to full strength and activity and would be responsible for the preparation of tactical units for combat
h   A General Headquarters, United States Army, would be activated as the high command of the field forces.

US officer cadets in a wartime graduation parade at West Point, have replaced their colourful full dress uniform with battle dress. However, they still carry the 1903 Model Springfield rifle, with bolt action and the long bayonet.

The basic elements of this mobilisation plan had of course been worked out pre-war, and in July 1940 a nucleus of GHQ had been established with the mission of speeding up the mobilisation process, by taking over the task of organising and training the field forces within the continental United States. This meant that Gen George C. Marshall, Chief of Staff, now had a second major post, as Commanding General of the Field Forces. However, it was a formal appointment only and Maj-Gen Lesley J. McNair, Chief of Staff at GHQ, really had active control, albeit on Marshall's behalf. As we shall see, the influence exerted by this remarkable officer on the buildup and continued reorganisation of all elements of the Army Ground Forces was considerable. Small in stature, he was both forceful and dominant. With the exception of Tank Destroyer battalions, he was a strong opponent of too much specialisation, believing that 'special type' units usually lacked basic military skills. He also hated waste of both men and equipment and was therefore constantly watchful and suspicious of any proposed new increase in unit Tables of Organisation and Equipment.*

The War Department had worked out a plan for activating divisions at a rate of three or four each month from March 1942. It was based on the cadre system (item d on page 9), experienced officers and men being drawn from an existing division to form the organising and training nucleus of a new one. They had first to be put through special training at the service schools and the divisional commander and his staff had to attend the Command and General Staff School, to prepare them for the onerous tasks which lay ahead. Most of the remaining officers would come direct from officer candidate schools and the enlisted men from replacement training centres. Gen McNair did not like this policy because he felt that new divisions should be built upon men who had at least completed their basic training, but such was the scale of expansion that this proved impossible to achieve. The War Department schedule allowed only 10-12 months for a division to be formed, staffed, equipped and trained to combat readiness (broken down into 17 weeks for establishing the initial organisation and completing the basic training programme; 13 weeks for unit training up to regimental level and finally about 14 weeks of combined tactical training, including at least one divisional level exercise).

As might have been expected with such a tight schedule, the Army had begun, by mid-1942, to meet some seemingly insurmountable problems. There were acute equipment shortages, so that divisions had to be activated with insufficient weapons for proper and realistic training. A system of priorities had to be worked out, with the categories A, B and C being allocated to units. Only those due for immediate shipment to a combat zone received priority A, which meant they got their full entitlement. B units received up to 50 per cent of their authorised quota

* Tables of Organisation and Equipment (T/O & Es) prescribed the standard form of units no matter where they were serving. This was essential for planning and procurement purposes. However, as units had to fight in various theatres of war under very different conditions, theatre commanders were authorised by the War Department to modify the tactical organisation and unit commanders on operations could rearrange their men and equipment to suit any particular set of circumstances.

and C units even less. On occasions units would be allocated priority A so close to their actual embarkation date that they did not have time to train with their new equipment. For example, bazookas were issued to units going on the Operation Torch landings without anyone knowing what they were for or how to use them! Despite these problems, the mobilisation proceeded at a cracking pace and by the end of 1942 virtually all the ground combat troops of the Army had been mobilised. Thereafter their striking power was only improved by economies and reorganisations from within themselves. In total the Army mobilised only 91 divisions (compared, for example, with 313 German, 120 Japanese, 550 Russian and 50 British) – just under 50 per cent of the original GHQ estimate. However, these divisions were all maintained up to strength throughout the war, despite casualties, no mean achievement when one realises that by early 1945, 57 infantry regiments in 19 different divisions had alone suffered between 100 per cent and 200 per cent casualties. Inevitably, changes in war plans resulted in long waiting periods before most of the newly formed divisions were 'blooded' in combat. With only one exception none of the divisions activated after Pearl Harbor entered battle before 1944.

TRAINING

Ground combat in World War II required many complex and technical skills. Even in the infantry a GI had to be able to use any of a dozen different weapons. He had to have a good knowledge of camouflage and concealment, of mines and booby traps, of patrolling, map reading, AFV and aircraft recognition, of how to use captured enemy equipment and how to deal with POWs, of field hygiene and first aid, of how to live rough for long periods under extremely difficult conditions. All these skills were vital to the soldier and as they were mainly military and not civilian skills, they had to be taught to new recruits from scratch. They also had to be taught how to become a member of a team, be it a rifle squad, a tank or gun crew. Mobile warfare required a high standard of physical fitness and mental alertness, whilst intelligence, skill and stamina were needed for both personal survival and eventual victory on the battlefield.

BASIC TRAINING

At the beginning of 1940 the only military training establishments in the USA were the General and Special Service Schools, small organisations with the task of training limited numbers of key individuals. The much larger task of giving basic training to all newly joined soldiers was left to units. Clearly this was an unacceptable system as far as the enormous influx of 'citizen soldiers' which the draft would produce. In 1940, therefore, the War Department adopted a new plan and special training organisations, known as Replacement Training Centres (RTC) were established all over America. The role of these RTCs was to provide a steady flow of trained men to tactical units, thus relieving those units of

'America trains men on mass production lines!' was the original caption for this staged 'battle' photograph. Note that all are armed with the 1928A1 model Thompson .45cal machine gun, with the old-type 50 round drum magazine, as they leap off two smoke-shrouded M2A2 light tanks (known as 'Mae Wests' because of their prominent twin turrets!).

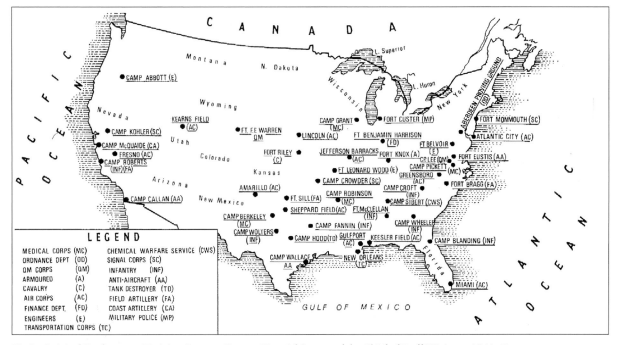

Fig 2 Original Replacement Training Centres. (Source: Biennial Report of the Chief of Staff US Army, 1941–3)

Gas-masked GIs jump from a Jeep during manoeuvres in Australia. Although respirators were issued to all ranks, fortunately gas was never used.

their training burdens during mobilisation and combat. Twelve ground force centres began to operate in March 1941: three for the Coast Artillery, one Armour, one Cavalry, three Field Artillery and four Infantry. During the rest of 1941 they trained over 200,000 men. After war was declared the RTCs had to fulfil two requirements: firstly to supply 'filler replacements' to occupy initial vacancies in units being activated or brought up to strength; secondly to provide 'loss replacements' for units already in training or engaged in combat. More RTCs were established to cover the new 'quasi' arms such as Anti-Aircraft and Tank Destroyer. Fig 2 shows the locations of the RTCs set up to train recruits for both the arms and services. They trained the newly inducted men in basic military subjects and in the elementary specialist techniques of their particular arm or service. The former included such subjects as military discipline, personal hygiene, first aid, guard duties and the care and use of personal weapons. Courses initially lasted for 12 to 13 weeks, but immediately after Pearl Harbor many RTC programmes were cut to 8 weeks. This did not last for long and by the autumn of 1943, with a few specialist exceptions, all courses had been fixed at a 17-week period.

SERVICE SCHOOLS

These were the agencies for training individual officers, officer candidates and enlisted specialists in the special skills of their arms. Between July 1940 and August 1945, nearly 570,000 men completed courses designed to fit them for a wide variety of jobs ranging, for example, from infantry battalion commander to anti-aircraft control technician. Eight schools operated under control of the Army Ground Forces, four (Cavalry, Coast

Artillery, Field Artillery and Infantry) had been in being for many years and were, until the March 1942 reorganisation, controlled by the chiefs of their respective arms. The remaining arms schools, established to teach new techniques, were Armoured, Anti-Aircraft Artillery, Tank Destroyer and Parachute. The last of these was really more than just a service school, as all airborne training required specialised training and thus the Parachute School had to train *all* parachute replacements; in effect it was thus both a school and an RTC.

OFFICER TRAINING

Officer candidates were trained and selected for commissions in an element of each of the service schools known as Officer Candidate Schools (OCS). The mission of the OCS was to convert enlisted men of the particular arm into combat officers to meet the mobilisation requirements which could not be filled by Regular, Reserve or National Guard officers. In courses varying from 12 to 17 weeks, the schools trained the candidates in the basic duties of a junior officer of their particular arm or service, and decided whether or not they were fit to be recommended for a commission. In 1942 they also took on the training of members of the Reserve Officers' Training Corps (ROTC) who had left college to enter the Army before completing their full ROTC course. This group represented about one-tenth of all OCS graduates from AGF schools and they received Reserve commissions after graduation. When the Army began to mobilise in 1940, it had only 14,000 professional officers, but by the end of 1943, when mobilisation was nearly complete, about 19,000 National Guard officers were in Federal service, some 180,000 officers had been drawn from the Officer Training Corps and nearly 100,000 civilians had received direct commissions – just under half as doctors, dentists and chaplains, the rest in technical and administrative posts. Three hundred thousand new officers had been commissioned from OCS or aviation cadets. There was continual agitation, especially by the Army Service Forces, to increase the length of the OCS course to six months, but this was never approved and no substantial changes were ever made to the course. AGF maintained that OCS provided only the initial and individual phases of officer training, which was then continued when he arrived at his unit. As the official history puts it: 'While AGF officer candidate schools fulfilled an indispensable mission, becoming the main source of junior officers, it was the combination of school and unit training that produced the successful junior officer for the ground combat arms in World War II.'

TACTICAL TRAINING

GHQ had developed a programme of tactical training which included the phases of small unit training (i.e. the coordination of the various weapons of the regiment and the division) and large scale manoeuvres. This programme remained virtually unaltered throughout the war and gave the World War II GI a much better preparation for combat than any of his

predecessors. The programme included proficiency tests at every stage, and an emphasis on elementary training and general proficiency as a prerequisite to specialist training. Manoeuvres were conducted with as few 'strings' as possible, with realistic battle simulation, meticulous umpiring and immediate debriefs so that the maximum amount of benefit could be gained by all taking part. A rough guide to the distribution of training time suggested for an infantry division was: 5 weeks for unit training, 4 weeks for combined training and 7 weeks for manoeuvres. These were preceded by a 13-week period of individual training and tests for replacements received from RTCs, and followed by a 6-week period of post-manoeuvre training. The directive which recommended this time scale also advised that if time did not allow for all these stages, then the most vital were the individual and small unit training, which must not be skimped.

US Army practising beach landings in the UK, prior to D-Day. Devon and Dorset were both used for practising large-scale landings, supported by aircraft and artillery.

C H A P T E R   3

HIGHER ORGANISATION

THE WAR DEPARTMENT

When Gen Marshall became Chief of Staff in 1939, he inherited a staff structure and a set of planning assumptions which were all hopelessly outdated. They had been formulated by a board set up in 1921 by Gen Pershing which was called the Harbord Board after its president, Maj-Gen James G. Harbord. In all their planning the board had used the basic assumption that any future war would be fought in a similar manner to World War I and would thus require similar command and management arrangements. Of course they could not have been more wrong and as a direct result the War Department had to struggle along in the period immediately before America entered the war (i.e. from 1939 to 1941), trying to adapt the Harbord Board concepts to a constantly changing world situation. When America did enter the war, Gen Marshall was determined to sweep aside the entire old-fashioned structure and to create a completely new one which would be capable of dealing with modern, global war.

The War Department organisation which he took over was still unchanged in June 1941. It was based upon outdated ideas, such as the assumptions that a war would be fought in one single theatre of operations and that the Chief of Staff would automatically take to the field as Commander in Chief. It was further anticipated that the President and the Secretary of War would follow World War I practice and delegate broad authority for conducting the war to the professional military officers. This also could not have been more wrong, because, like so many other Presidents before him, Roosevelt, as Commander in Chief of the Armed Forces of the United States, chose to play an active part and not to sit quietly on the sidelines. Indeed, he invariably dealt directly with Gen Marshall, rather than going through his Secretary of War, Henry L. Stimson, and Marshall's primary role became that of the President's adviser on military strategy and operations. This might well have led to friction between Stimson and Marshall, but fortunately this was not the case. After some initial problems they developed a close and deep relationship. A measure of this rapport is reflected in a remark made by the Secretary to Marshall at the end of the war when he said: 'I have seen many great soldiers in my lifetime and you, sir, are the finest I have ever known.'

By the end of their first 18 months of war – that is to say by June 1943 – the American war machine had grown to a size unparalleled in the nation's history. The strength of the Army alone had been increased by five million men. The scale of this expansion is hard to visualise, but as an example, the Army Air Force had been increased by 12,000 per cent and the Corps of Engineers by 4,000 per cent! This tremendous expansion necessitated a fundamental reorientation within the War Department and the way in which they did their business. Various services and supply agencies had to be integrated into the command organisation, so as to ensure not only the efficient assembling in the USA of all the means of waging war, but also to provide for its transportation and distribution to the combat areas overseas. As we have seen, an enormous training organisation was needed to train the ever growing citizen army, and for this to be done in an orderly and efficient manner, it had to be centralised under one authority. Early in 1942, after over a year of exhaustive study, a committee headed by Gen Joseph T. McNarney completed a plan for establishing three great commands under the direct supervision of the Chief of Staff. They were to be known as: the *Army Air Forces (AAF)*, the *Army Ground Forces (AGF)* and the *Services of Supply* later called the *Army Service Forces (ASF)*. Approved by the President and the Secretary of

Gen Eisenhower and his senior generals meet at Twelfth Army Group Headquarters, 12 May 1945. The photograph gives an excellent example of the diversity of even supposed 'standard' US Army uniforms! (via Patton Museum)

A Landing Craft Infantry about to beach on 'Bloody Omaha' on D-Day. Some excellent examples of combat uniforms and equipment can be seen among the GIs as they step off into the surf. (Their helmet patches – probably the divisional sign – have all been censored.)

War, the new organisation came into being on 9 March 1942 and is shown in Fig 3. To give some idea of the relative sizes of these three major elements of the American Army, let us examine the strength figures at the close of the war in Europe. In the summer of 1943 a firm decision had been made to build up the Army to an effective strength of 7,700,000 men. In 1945 the operating strength was 8,300,000 but this figure included 600,000 ineffectives. The ineffectives consisted of 500,000 men undergoing hospitalisation (including 100,000 in the process of being discharged because they were no longer fit for active or limited service), plus 100,000 en route overseas as replacements, making up the total of 600,000. The table below shows the breakdown of the 7,700,000 effectives between the AAF, ASF and AGF and the Theatre Forces, who were directly attached to the theatre HQs and major command installations worldwide; thus less than half the total Army manpower was actually employed as ground combat troops, the precise figures being as follows:

Army Air Forces	2,340,000
Army Service Forces	1,751,000
Theatre Forces	423,000
Army Ground Forces	3,186,000
Total:	7,700,000

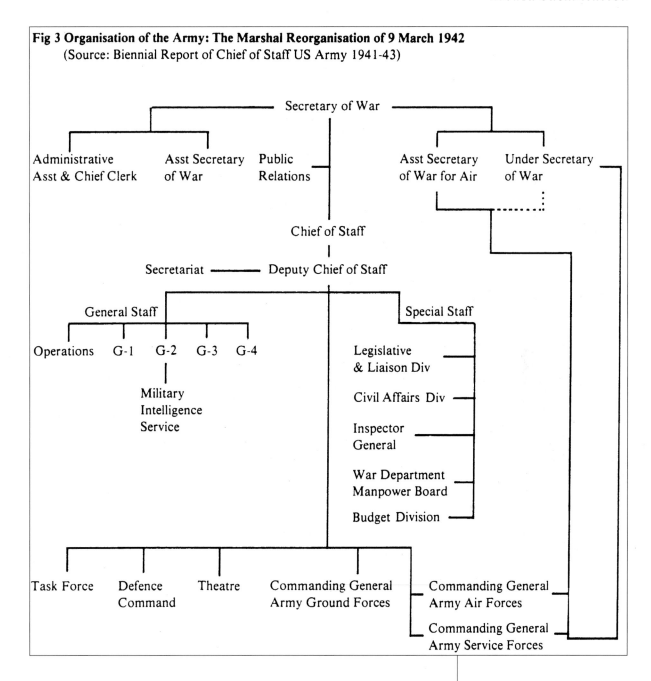

Fig 3 Organisation of the Army: The Marshal Reorganisation of 9 March 1942
(Source: Biennial Report of Chief of Staff US Army 1941-43)

ARMY AIR FORCES

As I am concentrating on the Army Ground Forces in this little book, there is no space to detail the organisation, role and tasks of the AAF, but clearly they cannot just be ignored. The 1942 reorganisation carried earlier air reorganisations to a logical conclusion, establishing them as an entirely separate command from the ground forces. They now had their own Air Staff, with its own chief, Gen Henry H. Arnold. Administering its own personnel and training, it organised and supported the combat air forces which were employed in all theatres of operations and came to exercise considerable influence over both strategic and operational planning. When World War II began in 1939,

Fig 3 Organisation of the Army: The Marshall Reorganisation of 9 March 1942. (Source: Biennial Report of the Chief of Staff US Army, 1941–3)

Over 3 million transport vehicles of all types were produced in the USA during World War II – here are just a few of them!

Infantrymen, tanks and 'Alligators' (amphibious tractors) clear out a village in Leyte, October 1944.

Tanks in line. The USA built a staggering 88,410 tanks between 1939 and 1945. These Shermans are being checked by an Ordnance officer in a US Supply Depot in the UK prior to D-Day.

the Army Air Corps, as it was then called, had a strength of fewer than 24,000 men. It eventually expanded to an air force of nearly 2.4 million! American industry produced nearly a quarter of a million aircraft, which were used to great effect, with 1,000 bomber raids over Germany and the fire bombing of Tokyo and Yokohama as but two outstanding examples of their air power. The culmination was of course the atomic bomb attacks which ended the war. It took another two years for the AAF to achieve completely separate and equal status, as the United States Air Force, with 'Hap' Arnold as its first five star general.

As far as the ground forces were concerned, the main types of air support given to them by the AAF were: close, direct fire missions on the immediate front of the ground troops; air defence of friendly forces and their installations in the combat zone; air attack against enemy targets in hostile rear areas; support for parachute and glider-borne operations; reconnaissance, liaison and observation.

ARMY SERVICE FORCES

I shall only deal in detail with those elements of the ASF operating with the combat troops and thus included in the 'Troop Basis' which was the laid down scale for apportioning men to the AGF. However, as with the AAF, it would be wrong to ignore the rest of the ASF, who were all commanded by Lt-Gen Brehon B. Somervell. They reached a peak size of 1,569,000 men and played a vital part in the successful prosecution

Bringing the supplies ashore at Iwo Jima. This cluttered beach shows how many and what variety of stores, vehicles and equipment was needed to supply US Army and USMC troops in the Pacific area.

of the war. A detailed list of their duties would be inappropriate and take up far too much space, but in summary they were responsible for: the supply, equipping and movement of troops both at home and overseas; for food, clothing, equipment, ammunition and the medical services; for road, rail and sea transportation; for personnel records and the mail service. In addition, they coordinated the production requirements of military munitions in the USA, the actual issue of weapons and equipment, plus everything else that affected the efficient and regular maintenance of this equipment; and the steady stream of supplies to all theatres of war. They were also responsible for many aspects of the troops' morale, such as film shows, educational programmes and newspapers. Their supply lines extended for over 56,000 miles and they had authority over the seven technical services, eight administrative services, nine corps areas (later called service commands), six ports of embarkation and nine general depots. HQ ASF were responsible for coordinating the work of all this varied array of agencies, and for the very first time full recognition was given to the vital importance of logistics and to the tremendous advantages which

Fig 4 Organisation of the Army Ground Forces. (Source: Biennial Report of the Chief of Staff US Army, 1941–3)

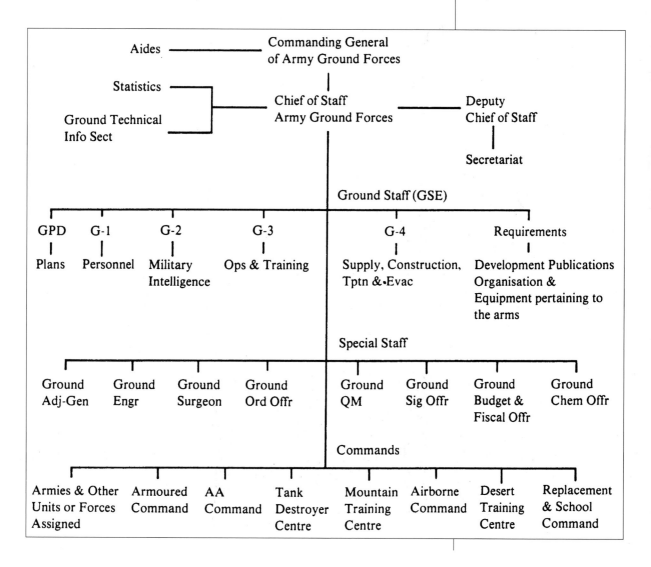

Gen Dwight D. Eisenhower, Supreme Commander of Allied Forces in Europe, in London, 12 June 1945, saluting the crowds as he drives to the Guildhall to receive the Freedom of the City.

could be gained by concentrating logistic operations in a single command. How well the ASF achieved their role can be measured by the fact that there were no *major* failures to supply during the war. Troops were successfully transported all over the world, and no battle or campaign was lost through a major logistic failure. Indeed, the GI was better supported than any other soldier in the war.

ARMY GROUND FORCES

The outline organisation of the Army Ground Forces, which is the real subject of this handbook, is shown at Fig 4. During the war HQ AGF administered 4,194,000 men and 230,000 officers. The ground forces suffered about 80 per cent of the American Army's battle casualties, were concerned in more than 40 major landings on enemy-held shores, and captured over 3½ million prisoners. A total of 92 divisions was activated before and during the war. In 1940, there were only eight Regular Army and Philippine divisions active, and between 1940 and 1942 a further 65 new divisions were activated. 90 divisions were prepared for combat and 88 of these were actually committed. Despite heavy casualties in some divisions, the AGF maintained them all at or near their correct strength.

STRUCTURE OF THE ARMY COMBAT TROOPS

Combat troops in the US Army were classified according to their weapons and to the method of combat they used: e.g. Infantry (ground and airborne), Armoured, Cavalry and Artillery (Field, Coastal and Anti-Aircraft). Combat troops were accompanied into battle by service troops who helped with supply, repair and administration, which thus freed the combat troops to get on with the actual fighting. Service troops included Engineers and Signals Corps, Transportation, Medical, Chemical, Finance, Ordnance, Military Police and Quartermaster troops. Personnel and administrative services were performed by the Judge Advocate General's Department (Legal), Special Services, the Corps of Chaplains and the Inspector General's Department.

C H A P T E R 4

NON DIVISIONAL UNITS, HEADQUARTERS AND THE STAFF

NON DIVISIONAL UNITS

Fewer than half of the tactical troops of the Army Ground Forces were actually organic to divisions; instead, they were in non divisional combat and service units. The ratio on 31 March 1945 was, for example, about 15:12 – 1,468,941 officers and men in non divisional units and 1,194,398 in divisions. There were also another 1,204,976 men in ASF type units in the Communications Zone (abbreviated 'Com Z'): the part of a theatre of operations behind the combat zone, where supply, transportation and other facilities are located and services performed. (See Fig 5 for an example of typical Com Z boundaries: North-West Europe, November 1944–January 1945). In March 1942, these non divisional units had been grouped at three levels, namely, Corps troops, Army troops and GHQ Reserve. Just in the

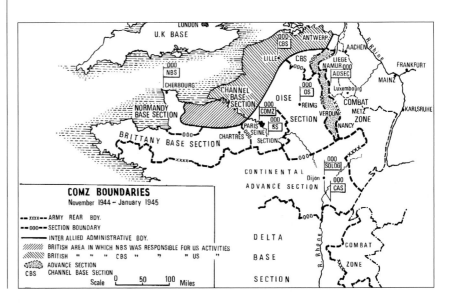

Fig 5   Com Z boundaries, an example from the ETO.

same way as each type of division had its laid-down organisation, so each corps and army had its own table of organisation which described what units there should be in a 'type corps' and 'type army' – see table below for details. The former consisted of three divisions, plus specified corps troops, whilst the latter contained three corps, plus specified army troops. Units not organic to divisions, corps or armies, were grouped into the theatre reserve.

The AGF were unhappy about this rigid system, feeling, rightly, that the 'type' concept set up false preconceptions with regard to tactical and logistical operations. What was needed was a far more flexible system, and although the plan which AGF subsequently put forward was never formally approved, it did go into effect piecemeal in 1943. This plan did away with organic corps and army troops, making *all* non divisional units part of GHQ Reserve. The only elements retained by corps and army were those over which they needed to exercise proper command: i.e. mainly headquarters and signal corps personnel. Troops were grouped in the smallest size compatible with efficiency, which was found to be the battalion. Corps and armies would then have these battalions of non divisional troops attached as necessary, the brigade and regimental

The standards of the Fifth Army, photographed at a Thanksgiving Service held at HQ Fifth Army on 9 May 1945.

Composition of the 'Type Army' and 'Type Corps', 31 July 1942
(Source: *US Army in World War II*, 'Organisation of Ground Combat Troops')

Branch	Type Army	Type Corps
	No Divs	3 Divs
AA	1 Bde	1 Regt
Armd	None	None
Cav	None	1 Mech Regt
Chem	1 Maint Coy	None
	1 Depot Coy	
	1 Impreg Coy	
	1 Lab Coy	
	3 Decon Coys	
Engr	3 Gen Serv Regts	2 Combat Regts
	6 Bns Sep	1 Corps Top Coy
	1 Depot Coy	
	1 Top Bn	
	1 Water Supply Bn	
	4 Lt Pont Coys	
	2 Dump Truck Coys	
	1 Cam Bn	
	1 Maint Coy	
	2 Hy Pont Bns	
Fd Arty	None	1 Bde
Inf	None	None
Med	3 Med Regts	1 Med Bn
	1 Vet Coy Sep	
	4 Surg Hosps	
	10 Evac Hosps	
	1 Conv Hosp	
	1 Lab	
	1 Supply Dept	
MP	1 MP Bn	1 MP Coy
Ord	2 Am Bns	1 Maint Bn
	1 Maint Bn	
QMC	3 MM Bns	2 Trk Coys
	1 MT Supply Coy	1 MM Coy
	1 Trk Regt	1 Gas Supply Coy
	6 Serv Bns	1 Serv Coy
	1 Gas Supply Coy	
	1 Car Coy	
	1 Ster Bn	
	1 Depot Coy	
Sig	1 Const Bn	1 Sig Bn
	1 Photo Coy	
	1 Pigeon Coy	
	1 Radar Int Coy	
	1 Op Bn	
	1 Depot Coy	
TD	3 TD Bns	1 TD Gp (5 Bns)
Aviation	1 Obsn Gp	4 Obsn Sqds

D-Day + 1. Red Beach HQ on Utah Beach, Normandy, 7 June 1944. (via Real War Photos)

levels ceasing to exist. (Regimental grouping *within* infantry divisions of course remained.)

In their place was put the 'Group'. In late December 1942, the War Department gave its approval to the plan to convert all non divisional regiments of anti-aircraft artillery, field artillery, mechanised cavalry and combat engineers into separate battalions, and to activate group headquarters in the ratio of one to each four/five battalions. Tank battalions, not in armoured divisions, and tank destroyer battalions already had the group system. Group headquarters were supposed to avoid administration, to be tactical only and to control their battalion in combat and in training. Battalions dealt directly with army on administrative matters, fetching their own supplies from army supply points.

HIGHER HEADQUARTERS

There were three levels of field command above division, namely Corps, Army and Army Group.

Corps

One of the main reasons for bringing in the 'battalion and group' system was to keep down the size of headquarters staffs, reducing the routine administration they had to deal with, thus keeping them as tactical as possible. This was certainly achieved with the corps HQ, as will be seen from the outline T/O & E 100–103 of 19 January 1945 below, with fewer than 200 men in the entire headquarters. Primarily a tactical unit, it was capable of controlling two or more divisions, plus whatever supporting and service units were needed for its particular mission. Some of these

Corps Headquarters			
(Source: *The Army Almanac*)			
Entire HQ	196	Judge Advocate-Gen's Sect	5
Commander and Aides	4	Finance Sect	8
Gen Staff Sect	60	Med Sect	9
Engr Sect	12	Ord Sect	18
Sig Sect	10	QM Sect	9
Chem Sect	5	Special Services Sect	4
Adj-Gen's Sect	28	Chaplain's Sect	6
Inspector-Gen's Sect	7	Public Information Sect	11

might be parcelled out to divisions straight away, the rest being kept under the corps commander's hand. By 1945 there were 24 active corps of which only one remained in the United States.

Army

The Field Army, to give its full title, was composed of an headquarters, two or more corps and such supporting and service units as were needed to achieve its mission. Unlike the corps, the army was both a combat and an administrative agency. In administration and supply it bypassed corps HQ

Mulberry Harbour. Half-tracks and jeeps using one of the Mulberry Harbours, built off the Normandy beaches to supply the assaulting armies.

To the Alps! GIs of 44th Inf Div, Seventh US Army, clear enemy out of the Austrian mountains, 29 April 1945.

and to a certain extent division as well. For the supply of food, fuel and ammunition, the AGF directive explained: '. . . division and corps are not in the channel of supply except for emergencies.' Both non divisional battalions and those in divisions were equipped with the necessary supply machinery which was supposed to 'mesh in' with that of army. Army pushed its supply points forward to positions which were easily accessible to the trucks of the user units. Army personnel sorted out the supplies into unit loads and put them on to the unit trucks. A great mass of administrative units was needed and to give some idea of the size and variety of these units Appendix Six at the end of the book gives the composition of the US Third Army in November 1943. The table gives an outline T/O & E of an army headquarters (T/O & E 200–103 of 26 October 1944). AGF kept the

Army Headquarters			
(Source: *The Army Almanac*)			
Entire HQ	778	Judge Advocate-Gen's Sect	9
Commander and Aides	7	Finance Sect	25
Gen Staff Sect	180	Med Sect	61
Engr Sect	72	Ord Sect	55
Sig Sect	73	Provost Marshal's Sect	9
Arty Sect	59	QM Sect	83
Chem Sect	26	Special Services Sect	3
Adj-Gen's Sect	91	Chaplain's Sect	7
Inspector-Gen's Sect	18		

number of army HQs activated to the minimum consistent with the tasks in hand. Initially, only the Second and Third Armies (plus four independent corps) were activated by AGF, while the Fifth, Sixth and Seventh Armies were all activated overseas, as were all the army groups and the First Allied Airborne Army. For a short time at the end of 1943 the Second, Third and Fourth Armies were in the USA, the Third (i.e. the HQ) then went overseas. No new armies were activated by the AGF until 1944, when the Eighth, Ninth, Tenth and Fifteenth Armies were activated and went rapidly overseas. Second and Fourth Armies remained in the USA, although strictly in name only, as the majority of the headquarters personnel went overseas under new army designations. By January 1945, not a single division was left in either the Second or Fourth Armies.

Army Group

When the forces in a theatre of operations consisted of several armies, then a headquarters called an Army Group was formed. It was the largest field organisation with a single commander, and its size could vary from about 500,000 to 1,500,000 men. The formation of army groups was primarily for tactical reasons, but also it was for ease of control, since it reduced the number of commanders with whom the theatre commander had to deal directly. The US Army formed only three army groups during the war – the 12th, commanded by Gen Omar N. Bradley, the 6th under Gen Jacob L. Devers and the 15th under Gen Mark W. Clark.

Eleven US divisions served with the Fifth (US) Army in Italy. Here are just a few of their infantry and AFVs congregating in the Piazza della Repubblica, Bologna, after the capture of the city on 21 April 1945.

The Staff

At the top of the headquarters of any corps, army or army group, was the commanding general – normally a major-general commanded a corps, a lieutenant-general an army and a full general an army group, but this did not always follow. Whatever his rank, like any other commander, he was ultimately responsible for everything that went on in his command. Directly under him was the chief of staff (COS) who was the CG's chief assistant and the coordinator of the staff. He, in turn, a deputy chief of staff. Beneath this 'top brass' were the staff, who comprised two basic groups, one consisting of the General Staff (five sections) and the other of the Special Staff (up to 18 different sections). Each of the General Staff branches was headed at army level, for example, by an assistant chief of staff in the rank of colonel, the Special Staffs by either colonels or lieutenant-colonels. The actual division was:

General Staff: G-1 Personnel; G-2 Intelligence; G-3 Operations; G-4 Supply; G-5 Civil Affairs and Military Government (including Displaced Persons).

Special Staff: Adjutant-general, artillery, anti-aircraft artillery, chaplain, chemical warfare, engineer, finance, HQ commandant, inspector-general, judge advocate, medical, ordnance, provost marshal, public relations, quartermaster, signal, special services and tank destroyers.

C H A P T E R   5

THE COMBAT ARMS

INFANTRY

'During World War II new terrains, new climates, strange weapons and unfamiliar peoples acted upon the American infantrymen. These destroyed thousands of men, put a lifelong mark on others, and changed somewhat the techniques of fighting on foot; nevertheless, in spite of everything, the basic characteristics of the infantry hardly shifted. Foot soldiers continued to be the only carriers of weapons who, in theory, were never exhausted, could always go another mile, and could be counted upon to move across any terrain in every quarter of the globe.' (US Army Lineage Series *The Infantry*.)

The coming of World War II resulted in the largest expansion of the US infantry ever seen. During the war years 1941–3, there was a 60 per cent

The team that got the job done. Infantry-tank cooperation was vital. Here, part of an infantry squad from 10th Inf Regt and a Sherman from 4th Armd Div are pictured near Bastogne.

increase and by the end of the war 317 regiments of infantry of various kinds had been activated. These included types of infantry never before seen in battle, such as the three mountain, 12 glider and 16 parachute regiments. In addition, there were 99 separate battalions, some of which had highly specialised roles. Among these were the six Ranger battalions, light infantry trained to cut deep into enemy-held territory and demoralise the foe in every way possible. The 1st Special Service Force was another commando-type organisation, designed to operate behind enemy lines in the snow covered terrain in Europe. Another was the 5307th Composite Unit (Provisional) which became famous under the nickname 'Merrill's Marauders' (after their commander Brig-Gen Frank D. Merrill) and operated in Burma along the Ledo Road. All soldiers in these special units were volunteers.

Another specialised type of infantry was that intended to provide the dismounted elements of the new armoured divisions, called appropriately 'armoured infantry'. They differed very little from the standard infantry soldier except that they had sufficient organic transport to move all ranks in one lift. However, unlike the motorised infantry of the shortlived motorised division, their vehicles were capable of cross-country movement and were also lightly armoured (i.e. they were halftracks). Several types of

Infantrymen of the 78th 'Lightning' Inf Div cleaning their personal weapons after 24 consecutive days of fighting across the Roer River, the Rhine and driving deep into the Remagen bridgehead, 28 March 1945. (via Real War Photos)

Taking cover behind a German anti-tank gun in Aachen, Pvt Wm Zukerbrow draws a bead on a Nazi sniper, 19 October 1944. (via Real War Photos)

light infantry were also tested, such as the mountain and jungle divisions. The final non standard infantry units were those in the airborne division, which were paratroops and glider infantry.

World War II American infantry included units made up exclusively of Americans of different racial or ethnic extraction. These included Indian, Negro, Puerto Rican and Filipino units, all of which had ample precedent; other separate battalions were added to this list, however, such as the 442nd Infantry who were American-born Japanese and the 99th Infantry Battalion of Norwegian Americans.

As well as massive expansion of manpower, World War II brought a bewildering increase in weapon technology, resulting in the infantryman having to be capable of using a wide variety of weapons, including mines, boobytraps, all types of grenades, bazookas and flame throwers, as well as more conventional small arms, mortars and machine guns. Battlefield communications improved out of all recognition and by the end of the war, eight radios were included in every rifle company, allowing them to stay in touch under the conditions of dispersion which the weight of enemy fire usually required. One of the most important new techniques which every infantryman had to learn was that of taking part in amphibious landings on hostile shores. Early in the war, they had to use whatever ships were available, but gradually purpose-built landing craft and amphibious vehicles, such as the DUKW, were developed.

ARMOUR

'Armor as the ground arm of mobility, emerged from World War II with a lion's share of the credit for the Allied victory. Indeed armor enthusiasts at that time regarded the tank as being the main weapon of the land army.' (US Army Lineage Series, *Armor – Cavalry*)

The bewildering success of the German armour with their blitzkrieg tactics of 1940 had a profound effect upon American military thinking on the way to use armour. It also led directly to the 'Armored Force' being created on 10 July 1940, with Brig-Gen Adna Chaffee as its commander. Under a week later 'I' Armored Corps was formed, consisting of the 1st and 2nd Armored Divisions, both of which were activated on 15 July. In addition, the 'Armored Force' had one separate non divisional tank battalion, the 70th. As the American Army grew in size so the number of armoured divisions and armoured corps naturally increased. 'II' Armored Corps was organised in February 1942, 'III' in August 1942 and 'IV' in September 1942. This was in line with the doctrine then current, that armoured divisions should be employed in special corps, composed of two armoured and one motorised divisions. By the end of 1943, however, this 'private army' approach had disappeared and armour was no longer treated as a separate force which should operate entirely on its own, but rather as a vital part of an all arms team. The Armored Force was

A Sherman of 13th Tank Bn, 1st Armd Div, attached to the 10th Mtn Div, motors through Verona, 26 April 1945.

Goodbye to Boots and Saddles! An M2A4 light tank overtakes a column of horse-mounted cavalry, during US Army manoeuvres held in the summer of 1940. The last horse-cavalry unit to fight mounted was the 26th Regiment of the Philippine Scouts in early 1942.

Shermans of an armoured unit practising for the invasion halt at sunset on a training area in the UK, 11 April 1944.

redesignated as the 'Armored Command' in July 1943 and then as the 'Armored Center' in February 1944. By then all armoured units had been assigned to corps and armies and the armoured corps redesignated as ordinary corps.

Non Divisional Tank Battalions

Between July 1940 and March 1943, 16 armoured divisions were activated, but this only accounted for part of the armoured strength of the army. There were in addition a large number of separate non divisional tank battalions; indeed by the end of 1944, they had reached a peak of 65, with another 29 in the course of formation. There were also 17 amphibian tractor battalions. Compared with these figures there were only 54 tank battalions in the armoured divisions. The majority of these separate battalions provided close support to the infantry divisions and their initial organisation was very similar to that of the infantry tank battalions of the interwar years. However, after the main army reorganisation they were put on to exactly the same organisation as those battalions in the armoured division, so that they were all completely interchangeable. This considerably simplified training, supply and reinforcement. The separate battalions were put under control of tank group headquarters, up to five battalions to each HQ. This proved to be too large a number and later was reduced to three. The system did not work all that well, as group HQ was just another HQ to complicate matters for the independent battalions, who were at times never quite sure under whose command they were meant to be! Some groups were expanded to include armoured infantry battalions and became called 'armored groups'.

Cavalry

I will deal with the two extant cavalry divisions later, as they do not count as mechanised troops. The rest of the cavalry do, as they were all eventually mechanised and served with distinction as 'recon' outfits with, for example, armoured and infantry divisions. There was a certain amount of reluctance to do away with the horse – there being more than 12 million horses and 4½ million mules in the USA at the beginning of the war – indeed, the last Chief of Cavalry, Maj-Gen John K. Herr said to a Congressional Committee in 1939 that horsed cavalry had: 'stood the acid test of war.' He also maintained that the best results could be obtained by using a mixture of horsed and mechanised cavalry. His office was eliminated, along with the other combat arms chiefs, when, in March 1942, the Army Ground Forces were formed and the trend towards complete mechanisation quickened. Some cavalry regiments were used to form the new armoured divisions, while all the remaining mechanised cavalry regiments were broken up in 1943, to form separate groups and squadrons. This reorganisation coincided with the new War Department principle to employ mechanised cavalry: 'to perform reconnaissance missions employing infiltration tactics, fire and manoeuvre.' Units were

Back to the cavalry! A detachment of the Provisional Mounted Reconnaissance Troop of the Fifth (US) Army passing through a shell-torn Italian mountain town.

organised and equipped to perform this role. The directive also specified that units were to engage in combat *only* to the extent necessary to accomplish their missions. This policy held for the rest of the war. During the war 73 non divisional cavalry units were active. In general they were squadrons and groups, many of which had been formed as explained above. Each mechanised group comprised an HQ and HQ troop, plus two or more recce squadrons. Groups were assigned to armies and mainly attached permanently to specific corps. In addition to the non divisional units there were also over 100 divisional cavalry units including an armoured recce battalion for each heavy armoured division and a cavalry recce troop for each infantry division.

The last horsed cavalry unit to fight mounted was the 26th Regiment of the Philippine Scouts, which in early 1942, after withdrawing to Bataan, was forced to destroy its horses and fight on foot. Of course both horses and mules were used as pack animals in the jungles and mountains, while a few special mounted recce troops were formed as and when required – for example the 3rd Infantry Division did so in Sicily and their Provisional Mounted Reconnaissance Troop was used for several months during the invasion of Italy. In September 1943 the troop had 143 horses and a pack train of 349 mules. Despite their mechanisation, it is interesting to note that cavalry units operated dismounted during combat almost twice as often as they did mounted. Also, despite their stated role, only 3 per cent of their active duty was concerned with pure recce tasks. The types of mission given and the frequency in which they were performed were given in the official history as: defensive missions 33 per cent; acting as a mobile service 29 per cent; security missions including blocking, screening, protecting flanks, etc. 25 per cent and offensive missions 10 per cent. For many of these missions a mechanised cavalry group would be reinforced with a field artillery battalion, a battalion of tank destroyers and a company of combat engineers.

Tank Destroyers

A major reaction in the USA to the German blitzkrieg was to look for a more effective means of stopping armour. The spectacular success of the German tanks was undoubtedly having a bad morale effect on the US combat troops and there was an urgent need for new and effective weapons to deal with them. The War Department decided that the answer was to use, en masse, fast moving high velocity guns. A few would be sited in static defensive positions, but the majority would be held as a mobile reserve ready to: 'seek, strike and destroy' enemy armoured thrusts. The new anti-tank battalions were called 'Tank Destroyers' to emphasise their aggressive role. The 'Tank Destroyer (TD) Center' was set up at Fort Meade, Maryland, then moved to a new camp at Fort Hood, Texas, in February 1942. Later that year the new TD force had reached a strength of nearly 100,000 men. It had 80 self-contained units each of 36 guns, plus strong recce and AA elements. About half the battalions were

Gun crew of the 598th Field Artillery, 92nd Inf Div prepare their 105mm howitzer for firing near the River Arno, Italy, in September 1944. (National Archives)

equipped with self-propelled guns, the rest with towed guns. SP tank destroyers were the M10 with a 3in gun, the M18 (Hellcat) with a 76mm and the M36 with a 90mm. The TD force went out of existence at the end of the war, because it had been found that a lightly armoured tank destroyer with its open turret was not as effective an anti-tank weapon as the better protected and armed tank.

ARTILLERY

'I do not have to tell you who won the war, you know our artillery did.' So said Gen George S. Patton, one of America's greatest battlefield commanders of the war. The service of artillery was divided between two arms known as the Field Artillery and the Coast Artillery Corps. The former manned and operated the artillery which accompanied the army into the field, while the latter manned and operated barrage balloons, the anti-aircraft artillery and the artillery and submarine mines used in the attack of enemy naval vessels. In the 1942/3 reorganisation, anti-aircraft artillery was separated from coast and became a 'Command' in its own right.

Field Artillery

Essentially a supporting arm, field artillery, which included light/pack, field, medium and heavy, was able to give close and continuous fire support to forward combat troops. It also gave support in depth with counter battery fire, fire on to enemy reserves, fire to restrict his movement in rear areas and to disrupt his command arrangements. It was able to deliver quickly, accurate fire of the right calibre and type of shell, on to a target under all conditions of visibility, weather and terrain, with or without adjustment (i.e. ranging). Artillery in World War II was far more technical and better controlled than ever before, with the perfection of the 'Fire Direction Center' (FDC) and the wide use of forward observers and spotter planes. The latter became standard in every division, thanks largely to Gen Eisenhower, who was a great advocate of this type of artillery fire control. The AGF continually tried to increase the amount of heavy artillery in proportion to medium artillery in order to create a more balanced force. It recommended in September 1942, 101 heavy battalions (equipped with 240mm, 8in and 155mm guns), plus 140 battalions of medium artillery (4.5in guns and 155mm howitzers), in addition to the medium artillery in divisions. The War Department reduced this bid to 81 medium and only 54 heavy battalions. This worried AGF considerably, but it was felt, with some justification, that at least part of the mission of heavy artillery could be performed by air bombardment. However, in July 1943 an increase was authorised of heavy battalions from 54 to 77. As late as January 1944 only 61 were active and some of these were in a very early stage of training. AGF 'returned to the charge' and finally the War Department authorised a further 30 battalions, making a total of 111 heavy battalions. By then the number of divisions had been cut to 90; thus the proportion of medium to heavy and to divisional strength was at an

Future artillery officers at an OCS on the East Coast of the USA load a Bofors 40mm AA gun.

acceptable level, although it was still only two-thirds of the original recommended 'ideal'. All field artillery heavier than 155mm was of course pooled above divisional level, as were a considerable number of medium and lighter pieces.

Anti-Aircraft Artillery

Originally 800 battalions of AA artillery had been planned, but this figure was reduced to 575 in October 1943. Even after this reduction it is interesting to note that AA artillery still had an authorised strength nearly *four* times that of non divisional field artillery (AA increased 1,750 per cent in three years from 31 December 1940, while field only increased 500 per cent). There were difficulties over training, particularly because of the wide dispersion of training centres and the need to produce so many units. In operational theatres AA guns brought down a good number of enemy planes, but also fired frequently on friendly aircraft, the result of rushed training. This situation was not helped by the undoubted success of AA guns in their secondary role against ground targets, which meant even more complex training. A specially appointed board, which followed the shooting down of US planes in Sicily in 1943 by friendly guns, recommended that AA training should be transferred to the AAF, but this was disregarded by the War Department. Eventually AA battalions were reduced, 100 being inactivated, until the total strength fell to 460 battalions by 1944. 'Many of the AA troops whose training had caused such concern wound up in the infantry.' (*US Army in World War II*, page 423 of 'The Organisation of Ground Combat Troops'.)

Coast Artillery

The Coast Artillery Corps manned and operated all fixed artillery, all railway artillery, all tractor-drawn artillery assigned for coast defence purposes, all controlled mine installations, all underwater sound ranging installations and, until reorganisation, all AA artillery, searchlights, power plants, communications, transportation and other accessories required for the maintenance and tactical employment of these weapons. In addition it operated barrage balloons. Its mission was the attack of enemy naval vessels by artillery fire and submarine mines and the attack of enemy aircraft by ground fire. Coastal artillery regiments were broadly classified as 'Mobile' or 'Harbor Defense'. The former were armed with either 155-mm guns or 14-in railway guns, the latter were assigned to a particular harbour to man its defences. The Mine Planters Service formed a part of the corps as did anti-motor torpedo boat units.

C H A P T E R 6

THE SERVICES

When the Army was reorganised in 1942, the Technical Services were grouped under the Army Service Forces, but they did have many elements within the AGF which were included in the Troop Basis, and thus considered as combat troops. Indeed, there was a strong body of opinion that felt some of them – e.g. the Corps' of Engineers and Signals – should be considered as 'Arms' and not 'Services' (cf the British Army). However, as this is the way they were officially grouped, then this is the way I shall deal with them, although I shall concentrate on the elements found in the AGF. The seven technical services to be covered are therefore: Engineers, Signals, Chemical Warfare, Quartermaster, Ordnance, Medical and Transportation, but first a few general words on the subject of supplies.

For planning purposes and distribution, supplies were considered in five classes:

Class 1   Those generally used up at a regular rate, regardless of conditions, principally food.
Class 2   Items (including clothing, weapons, etc.) for which there was a laid down scale of entitlement by units and individuals.
Class 3   All classes of petrols, oils and lubricants, known collectively as 'POL'.
Class 4   A miscellaneous category to cover everything not covered elsewhere.
Class 5   Ammunition, explosives and chemical agents.

Although the requirements of the different theatres varied with local conditions, it took an average 1,600 tons of supplies daily to maintain a divisional 'slice' consisting of a full strength division, plus a proportional share of all the necessary supporting and service troops, plus two air wing 'slices', making a total of 500,000 men in all. The 1,600 tons was broken down into: 1,100 tons of all types of dry cargoes, 475 tons of bulk petroleum products and 25 tons of vehicles. Out of this total 595 tons went to the combat zone for ground forces, 65 tons for air forces and 365 tons went up to the divisional area. There was a good deal of variation in lb/day between theatres in the various classes of supplies, but the total remained about the same: 66.81lb per man in Europe and 67.4lb in the Pacific. In Europe this included 7.7lb of rations, 0.426lb of clothing and equipment, 7.821lb of construction materials and 3.64lb of ammunition. In the Pacific the amounts were: 6.71lb rations, 1lb clothing and equipment, 11.9lb construction

Trucks and jeeps offload supplies onto mule transport in a mountain village in Italy. Wheeled vehicles could go no further, so it was mule or manpack.

materials and 5.14lb ammunition. As in World War I there was a tendency to overequip the GI which led to unnecessarily high transport demands. Various novel ways of ensuring that the supplies got through were used, such as the 'Red Ball Express' system in the ETO (European Theatre of Operations). This involved operating a one-way loop highway system, in which roads were exclusively reserved to Red Ball vehicles. It was very successful, reaching a peak on 29 August 1944, when 132 truck companies, running 5,958 trucks, carried 12,342 tons of supplies. In some instances, air supply was used most successfully, such as when Third Army had pushed into Austria and Czechoslovakia, some 22 per cent of all POL (six million gals) and 11 per cent of all rations went by air between 30 March and 8 May 1945.

The supplies must go through! A Filipino woman ignores a convoy crossing a pontoon bridge over the Pampagna River en route for Manila, March 1945.

FRONT LINE RESUPPLY

For normal day to day resupply, most front line companies depended on the nightly arrival of jeeps and trailers, usually under cover of darkness in the evening, when in contact, enemy activity and terrain permitting of course! They would bring up the rations, water, radio batteries, dry socks, etc. An ammunition resupply was also likely at the same time, although the battalion ammunition and supply platoon usually maintained an ammunition point from which ammunition could be collected any time. Most commanders liked to send up hot meals whenever possible, in

Black GIs unload drums of gasoline at the West Moors POL (petrol, oil and lubricants) Dump, Dorset, UK on 22 November 1943.

containers (called 'Marmite cans') which kept the foot hot, platoons and squads rotating back to a suitable location to eat. More and more frequently however, units had to depend upon daily issues of 'K' or 'Ten in One' rations (see Chapter Eight). They were of course designed to be eaten hot or cold. Men would try to find some form of shelter where they could make a fire to brew up the instant coffee or chocolate drinks. When it was impossible to reach forward troops by jeep, the reserve companies, HQ platoons, etc., would porter them forward. Fig 6 shows diagrammatically, ammunition and ration resupply procedure for an infantry battalion.

ENGINEERS

'The primary mission of engineers in our Army is to increase the combat power of our forces by construction or destruction which facilitates the movement of friendly troops or impedes that of the enemy. Engineers give technical assistance to other arms in construction of protective works, in camouflage, and by supply and maintenance of certain equipment and materials. They engage in combat when necessary.' That is how the wartime *Engineer Field Manual* (FM 5–6) explained the mission of combat engineers. On 30 June 1939 there were only 786 engineer officers and 5,790 enlisted men in the Regular Army. Only about 200 of the

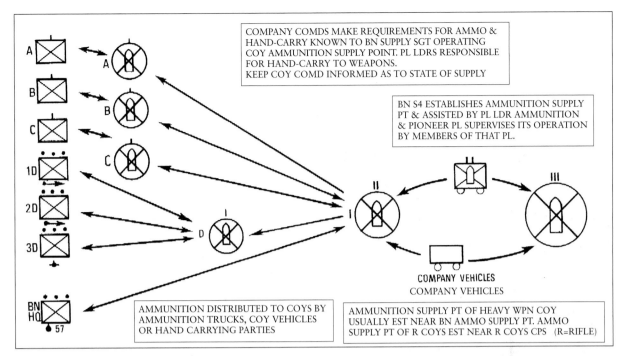

Fig 6   Resupply: a: Ammunition Distribution

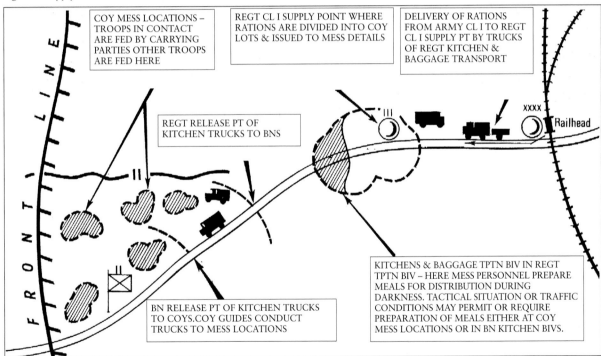

Fig 6   Resupply: b: Ration Distribution

officers were on duty with troops in the field, the rest being in staff jobs. By June 1940 there had been little change, with 44 reserve officers being called to active duty while the enlisted men had increased to 9,973. However, as the official engineer history points out: '. . . this was a mere trickle. Within the next year the flow turned into a raging torrent'. By December 1943 its strength was 561,066 and the corps reached its peak in

Engineers had many jobs to perform, one of the least glamorous being road-building and maintenance, such as seen here in Italy.

May 1945 when there were 688,182 engineers, representing 8 per cent of the Army. Greater in strength than any of the other technical services, the engineer procurement programme reached its peak in December 1944, when 190 million dollars worth of supplies were delivered. As there were engineers in both the AGF and ASF, there were frequent command problems on who should control engineer units. On paper the division appears simple, combat units with AGF, service units with ASF and AAF. The trouble was that service units were often employed in both combat and service zones. In January 1943 the division of control was laid down as follows:

Armed Ground Forces

Special amphibian bdes	Camouflage bns and coys
Combat regts and bns (armd, mot, airborne and mountain)	Topographic bns (army) and coys
	Water supply coys
Heavy pontoon bns	Depot coys
Light pontoon bns	Maintenance coys

Army Service Forces

General and special service regts	Port construction and repair gps
Separate bns	Topographic bns (GHQ)
Dump truck coys	Equipment coys
Forestry coys	Base shop coys
Petroleum distribution companies	Heavy shop coys

This list gives a good indication of the scope of engineer activities, while Appendix Five gives details of actual strengths of engineer units at the end of the war. As this table shows, about 40 per cent of the corps were serving with AGF, 40 per cent with ASF and the remaining 20 per cent with AAF. However, the distinctions between AGF, ASF and AAF engineers broke down in the war theatres, whatever engineers there were available being used to get the job done. Front line engineers had to clear and construct obstacles, lay minefields, ferry troops across rivers, build bridges and, when the necessity arose, fight as infantry. Those in the rear were more concerned with building shelters, roads, ports and airfields, and with supply functions. By June 1945, 89 divisional combat battalions, 204 non divisional combat battalions, 79 general service regiments and 36 construction battalions had been mobilised. Flexible grouping began in early 1943, when the AGF brought in the 'group' system, an engineer combat group HQ controlling two/three separate combat battalions.

Bridge-building had to take place no matter what the weather. Some very wet engineers building a pontoon bridge, somewhere in Italy in 1944.

Divisional Engineers

The combat engineer battalion in the infantry division grew from 634 to 745 men in 1941–2. This was reduced by the AGF to 647. Functions, such as road repair, bridge building, etc. were left unchanged. A recce section was added to battalion HQ and service company, so that the CO could formulate his own estimates for bridging or road repairs. The main way the size was reduced was by removing certain items of bridging equipment, to be held at a higher level, together with more engineers (e.g. heavy and light pontoon units) who were then available to support the divisional engineers as necessary. In the armoured division the 1942 armoured engineer battalion had four companies and a treadway bridge company, but AGF reduced this by 40 per cent (from 1,174 to 693). The treadway bridge company was removed and made a non divisional army unit, the four general engineer companies were reduced to three. This was done to bring the battalion down to the size of that in the infantry division, because AGF felt it was inconsistent for armoured exponents to argue about the ability of tracked vehicles to move off the roads and simultaneously demand more engineers to deal with more frequent road repairs caused by the same AFVs!

SIGNALS

In line with the rest of the Army, the Signal Corps was short of both men and materials as the war clouds grew. In the summer of 1939 its strength was under 4,000, although by the time America entered the war this had been gradually built up to 3,119 officers and 48,344 men. However, they were scattered throughout the continental USA, the Caribbean, Greenland, Iceland, Newfoundland, Hawaii, Philippines and even Alaska. An enormous expansion was necessary, when one considers that the triangular infantry division alone included 1,500 communications men – about one

A lineman at work in France, tightening a 'messenger' cable before fastening it to a pole.

tenth of the divisional strength – despite the fact that they were not all Signal Corps, they still all needed communications training. Industrial support was also lacking and there was no experience in the mass production of precise military radio and radar equipment, so an enormous organisation of skilled men had to be built up. 'We were walking on unchartered ground', wrote the Assistant Chief Signal Officer, 'we had no pattern to follow either in organisation or demands.' The Signal Corps developed, supplied, installed and maintained its specialised equipment, not only for the AGF and ASF, but also for the AAF, who needed even greater quantities of highly complex communications equipment. The radio sets of the US ground forces were the envy of all the Allies and were never bettered throughout the war by any other nation. Long-range mobile sets such as the SCR299 and SCR399 were widely prized, while the short-range vehicular FM radios provided the GI with unrivalled interference-free voice communications.

Under the 1942/3 reorganisation the Signal Corps, like the Engineers, was assigned to the ASF. There were natural and valid objections to this; for example, in other armies signal control enjoyed a place in the high command structure; the reorganisation overlooked the fact that the Signal Corps was both an arm and a service; and finally, that signal communications were one of the major functions of command.

The estimate of manpower requirements made on 1 July 1943 was for 60,000 men for each ASF and AGF and 41,000 for the AAF. A revision in October 1943 put the ASF–AGF figures up by 17,000 and decreased the AAF requirements slightly. However, at that late stage in mobilisation there was no hope of finding the extra manpower. In July 1943 the Corps strength was 27,004 officers and 287,000 enlisted men, and by 1 May 1945, the total strength had reached 321,862 (3.9 per cent of the Army), which represents a Signal Corps 54 times larger than it had been in 1940.

Combat Units

Within the AGF there were three times as many signal troops in non divisional units as in the divisions. This was because, as I have already explained, a large proportion of signal equipment in a combat arm was manned by members of that particular arm. The Signal Corps units in a typical field army comprised only about 3½ per cent of the total force. In addition to signal companies, units included: an HQ signal service company; a signals operation battalion, which furnished communications at the army command posts; one or more construction battalions making telephone cable and wire installations down to corps level and back to army rear HQ; one or more signal radio intelligence companies; a pigeon company and a signal photographic company. Finally, there were a signal repair company and signal depot company which dealt with the supply and maintenance functions of the field army. These troops were often augmented by special detachments of various types. During their 281 days of campaigning Third Army Signallers laid over 16,000 miles of telephone wire, rehabilitated 4,000 miles of French and German wire and over 36,000 miles of underground cables. Their Message Centre alone handled a total of

7,220,261 code groups, while forward and rear echelon switchboard operators handled an average of nearly 14,000 calls *a day*! The divisional signal company increased in strength from 232 in 1940 to 322 by March 1942. It was then reduced by almost one-third on reorganisation, down to 226 all ranks. This was done by eliminating truck drivers and making the specialists drive themselves, and also by the transfer of the radio intelligence platoon to corps.

CHEMICAL WARFARE

The Chemical Warfare Service (CWS) provided units in all the theatres of war during World War II. In 1940 the CWS had an active strength of just 93 officers and 1,035 enlisted men with an appropriation of one million dollars. By 1943 its strength had risen to 8,103 officers and 61,688 men, while the budget exceeded one billion dollars. Initially their reason for being was to defend against an enemy gas attack and to be ready to retaliate efficiently. This meant having defensive chemical warfare material, such as gas masks and protective clothing, plus offensive material, like toxic agents and the necessary munitions and weapons to deliver them. Fortunately World War II proved to be a non-gas war, but the need to be always prepared was present throughout. Instead of gas other chemical weapons were used – e.g. large and small area smoke weapons, flamethrowers and incendiary devices. There were many different specialised CWS units, such as chemical laboratories, decontamination, processing, maintenance and service companies. However, the CWS units with whom the combat troops mostly came into contact with were:

a. Smoke generator companies – first saw service in NW Africa, providing screens at the entry ports during the Operation Torch landings. The M1 mechanical generator was used, which produced not smoke, but an artificial fog, by the condensation of water and oil. The main drawback of the M1 was its weight (3,000lb) but in 1944 a small compact model, the M2 was produced.
b. Chemical mortar battalions – armed with the 4.2in mortar capable of firing toxic chemical and smoke bombs, it was given an HE mission as well. Few in number and greatly overworked, the CW mortar battalions served as the infantry commander's 'hip pocket artillery', capable of placing accurate and heavy fire on targets up to about 5,000-yd range.
c. Portable and mechanised flamethrowers – these were employed with mixed success, by combat troops. Certainly they were more useful in the Pacific theatre, where the stubborn and determined enemy had often to be burnt out of its positions, after mortars and artillery had proved ineffective. The jungle also helped the firer to get close enough to use his easily recognisable weapon without being seen.

THE QUARTERMASTER CORPS IN THE COMBAT DIVISION

The division was the smallest combat formation at which the Quartermaster Corps (QMC) was provided for infantry, cavalry and airborne divisions. In armoured divisions, less the 2nd and 3rd Armored Divisions who kept their QMC battalions, all lost their integral battalions retaining only the divisional staff. The strength of the QM company in the infantry division was 186 and consisted of three truck platoons and a service platoon. Each truck platoon (1 officer and 28 men) operated 16 X 2½ ton trucks, which drew Class 1 and Class 3 supplies daily from army truckheads and distributed them to vehicles of the combat units at divisional distribution points. The service platoon (1 officer and 48 men) manned the distribution point and transferred the supplies. Whenever possible, men of the service platoon also went with the trucks to the army truckheads to help load supplies as this saved valuable time, and it was time not tonnage which was the main limiting factor in all QMC truck operations. Using trucks going back to collect rations for such extra purposes as evacuating POWs and salvage, was clearly necessary, but did put an extra strain on drivers. Relief drivers could seldom be found, certainly not from the service platoon which had to collect salvage, sort laundry, operate showers, assist grave registration units and perform a hundred and one other vital jobs. During combat, when supply lines

Drivers of the 5th QMC Company of the 5th Inf Div stand by their trucks ready to move out. Note the ring-mounted .50s on the roofs of some vehicle cabs. (via Real War Photos)

lengthened and thousands of other combat troops were attached to divisions, the organic QM company just couldn't cope alone, so whenever possible the corps loaned extra troops from its service company to help the hard pressed divisional company. In the ETO, each armoured division had two QM truck companies attached when in combat. One company was primarily used for ammunition, the other for all other classes of supplies, including POL. The armoured division usually needed about twice as many POL as infantry divisions, but as the complete division was motorised, a large number of organic vehicles drew their POL direct from army Class 3 truckheads. Until late 1944, the QM company of the airborne division had a strength of only 87 and comprised an HQ, service platoon and an airborne truck platoon of jeeps and trailers. For ground combat after link up, a standard truck company was normally attached. In late 1944 the company was increased to 11 officers and 197 enlisted men. What this really amounted to was the permanent combination of the old airborne QM company and the attached truck company.

Undoubtedly all QMC companies were overstretched throughout the war and there were constant calls for increases. One of the strongest was from the QM of Third Army, who called for the expansion of the divisional company to a battalion of two truck companies and a service company. The proposal included specialised manpower for ration breakdown, POL distribution and for providing baths, laundry, salvage and repair services. Despite the fact that these proposals were supported by a score of battle tested divisional QMs, they were rejected by the War Department, due to 'personnel limitations'. QM units in the ETO included specialist units such as bakeries, gasoline supply, graves registration, laundry, refrigeration, salvage, sterilisation, fumigation and baths, and war dogs.

ORDNANCE

To keep the tanks, halftracks, trucks and all the other vehicles rolling, there had to be in each division a special unit to back up unit fitters. In the armoured division this was the Ordnance Maintenance Battalion, in the infantry division the Ordnance Light Maintenance Company. Battlefield recovery of disabled equipment was a unit responsibility as were elementary repairs and maintenance. Units were expected to carry out third echelon maintenance to the very limit of their tools and the skill of their fitters. Indeed, rather than lose control of their own vehicles by turning them over to another agency, units were perfectly happy to do this. Thus, the ordnance unit as provided in the AGF tables was deliberately designed to undertake only 60 per cent of the third line repairs required during quiet periods and only 30 per cent during combat. The infantry division company was only 147, as compared with 762 all ranks in the much more mechanised armoured divisional battalion.

Medical

In all divisions the medical personnel were divided into two types: firstly there were those attached medics who were a permanent part of all major units and provided the immediate first aid and casualty evacuation to

Ordnance fitters at work, using the lifting tackle fitted to their Ward La France 626 6 ton wrecker, to lift the radial engine of this Sherman tank.

battalion or regimental aid stations. They were backed up by the other type, the medical battalion. (The airborne division had only a strong company.) If one takes the infantry division for example, there were about 1,000 medical personnel, less than half of whom were in the medical battalion. Medical battalion personnel assisted the unit-attached medics to collect wounded and to bring them to unit aid stations. They also evacuated the wounded on up the chain to clearing stations and then on to the evacuation hospitals which operated at army level. Divisional MOs worked at clearing stations during operations or reinforced unit MOs. On reorganisation in 1942/3, an additional clearing platoon was added to the clearing company, so that one could be attached to each of the three regimental combat teams in the triangular division. There were more medical personnel in the infantry division than any other arm or service except for infantry and artillery.

Medical evacuation within the combat zone was by litter, jeeps and ambulances. Air evacuation might be possible by liaison plane or light transport. Surface evacuation from the combat zone (CZ) was the responsibility of the CZ commander, be it by road, rail or sea. Types of hospitals usually allocated to armies included evacuation, convalescent and portable surgical. In the CZ there were field, convalescent, station and general hospitals. The 'neck of the funnel' were the evacuation hospitals through which all casualties (less those by air) had to pass on their way to hospitals in the communications zone (ComZ). They were located about

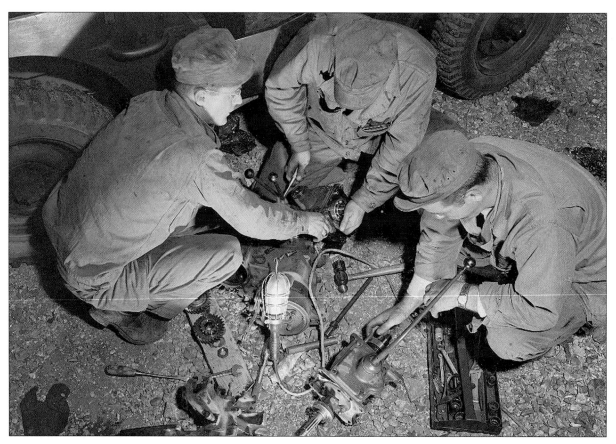

Ordnance fitters working on damaged jeep transmissions in the UK, so that they can repair vehicles which must leave for France in three hours, 24 July 1944.

An MO tends a wounded man, hit by a sniper near Carentan, June 1944, while a GI stands guard with his Thompson sub-machine gun. The doctor wears the insignia of the 9th USAAF on his arm.

A wounded GI receives a blood transfusion just half a mile behind the front line in Sicily, as Sicilian peasants look on.

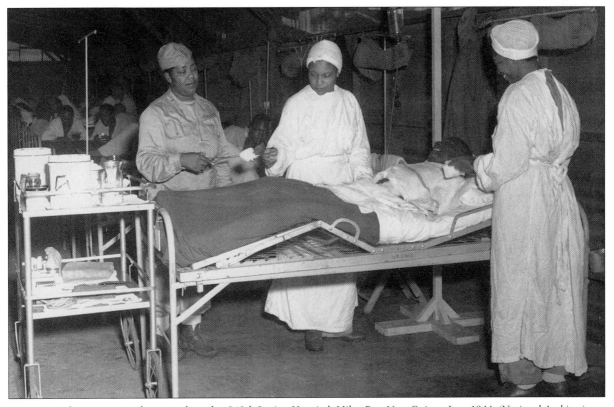

Nurses provide treatment in the surgical ward at 268th Station Hospital, Milne Bay, New Guinea, June 1944. (National Archives)

A UK-bound LCI being loaded with wounded from ambulances, Normandy, August 1944. (via Tank Museum)

Padre giving communion beside an artillery gun in France, 1944.

Unloading an ammunition train onto waiting 'Deuce and a halfs' at a railhead near Brest, during the siege of the town in August 1944. (via Tank Museum)

Bound for UK. A full shipload of 15,000 GIs on board RMS Queen Mary sets off from New York. It was 'standing room only' on deck, when all of them tried to get a farewell glimpse of home!

12 to 30 miles from the battle front, on good roads and near airfields, railways and waterways. Portable surgical hospitals, of 25 beds, were first developed in the South-West Pacific in 1942 and were mobile units used to reinforce divisional clearing stations by providing immediate surgical treatment for patients too seriously wounded to be moved to the rear. Patients who were short term usually remained at convalescent hospitals in the army area. Field hospitals were mobile hospitals, capable of giving station hospital type of service in the field whenever there was a temporary need. Station hospitals were fixed units which served a limited assigned area only. They did not usually receive patients from the combat zone. General hospitals were also fixed units of 1,000, 1,500 or 2,000 beds capacity, equipped to give complete treatment for all cases in the theatre. Most patients could be expected to come from the combat zone. Air evacuation to the USA was the responsibility of Air Transport Command, but the ComZ had to arrange for the patients' arrival at airfields and care for them until they caught the plane.

The chief surgeon of the theatre prepared the general plan for evacuation and hospitalisation of the sick and wounded. The system was based upon the premise that it was the responsibility of rearward units to relieve forward units of their casualties; there was also a laid down number of days that patients should be held in a particular theatre for treatment before evacuation to the USA. These were: 90 days for the South-West Pacific, South Pacific and North Africa (because of the lack of hospital facilities); 180 days for Europe and all other theatres (later reduced to 120 days).

TRANSPORTATION

Prior to March 1942, there was a Transportation Division under the Quartermaster General and certain separate field installations that reported directly to the Chief of Staff, such as ports of embarkation, holding and reassignment points, which handled all domestic and overseas movement of both men and materials. Gen Somervell, CG ASF, was determined to merge all these units into a single operating agency. It was initially called the Transportation Service. This still left water transportation with the QM Corps and overseas railways with the Engineers. In July 1942, this was officially approved and the Transportation Corps, under a Chief of Transportation, was created with its own branch insignia. In November 1942, 17 railway operating and maintenance units were redesignated as part of the Transportation Corps.

CHAPTER 7

DIVISIONAL ORGANISATIONS

The division can best be described as the smallest composite unit which is capable of operating completely independently. During World War II there were three main types of division – infantry, armoured and airborne. Other specialised divisions were – cavalry, motorised and light (including mountain). Of the 89 divisions in existence at the end of the war there were 66 infantry, 16 armoured, five airborne, one mountain and one cavalry. If the non divisional units of infantry and artillery were also grouped together they would have amounted to nearly another six infantry divisions, while doing the same with the various independent armoured units would have assembled a further 20 armoured divisions. Each of the main types of division was normally reinforced beyond its standard establishment with sufficient units of the arms and services so as to ensure that it could fulfil its battle mission. These might include tank destroyers, AA artillery, chemical weapons, truck companies, engineer treadway bridge companies, field hospitals, ambulance companies, signal photo companies, counter intelligence and interrogation of POW teams, etc.

Tables of Organisation and Equipment

In describing the various organisations I shall refer to the tables of organisations and equipment (T/O & Es), which prescribed the standard form of units no matter where they were stationed. It was obviously necessary to have a standard organisation for planning and procurement purposes, but clearly the circumstances in which divisions had to fight in the various theatres of war were vastly different. Theatre commanders were therefore authorised by the War Department to modify the tactical organisation and unit commanders on operations were able to rearrange their men and equipment to suit any particular set of circumstances. Standard units prescribed in T/O & Es (normally called T/O units) were designed to be adequate in any conditions, requiring the minimum of battlefield reorganisation by commanders. They were designed to the do the job with no more men and equipment than was absolutely necessary. T/O & Es were amended from time to time in the light of experience gained in battle.

AN ARMOURED DIVISIONAL HEADQUARTERS IN ACTION

In his book *The Super Sixth*, George F. Hofmann gives this description of an armoured division HQ in action:

Division HQ Company provided the administrative, supply and service personnel and the local security for both Forward and Rear Echelons of Division Headquarters. The Forward Echelon included the Division Commander, Assistant Division Commander, their aides and the liaison officers from subordinate and adjacent headquarters, Chief of Staff, Assistant Chiefs of Staff G-1, G-2, G-3 and G-4, Division Surgeon, Signal and Engineer Officers (the latter also commanded the 25th Engineers and was usually represented by an Assistant Division Engineer). The Division Chemical Officer and Military Government Officer joined the Forward Echelon when appropriate. G-1, G-4 and the Division Surgeon rotated between Forward and Rear Echelon as the situation demanded. Forward Echelon was located, both on the march, in combat or in bivouac, as far forward as practicable to facilitate communication and personal contact with combat units. The Division Commander or the Assistant Division Commander, their aides and, from time to time officers from the G-2 and G-3 sections, constituting an 'advance party', kept in close personal touch with the 'main effort' during combat and at the same time, in radio touch with the Division CP where the Chief of Staff, in touch with all units through radio, wire or liaison personnel, kept the Commander informed and issued orders as directed or, if necessary, on his own, in accordance with the plan. The magnificent communication facilities rarely failed to keep all commanders and staff personnel in touch.

The Headquarters Commandant with the security platoon was charged with moving, locating and protecting the Division CP as directed by the Chief of Staff. On rapid advances, this frequently took the party under fire as they sought a forward position in anticipation, usually proven justified, of continued advance.

The Rear Echelon was under control of the Division Trains Commander for movement and security. The latter duty often fell to the Band as well as the MP Platoon. In addition to HQ and HQ Company of Division Trains, the following sections of Division HQ, constituting the Rear Echelon, were normally present: The Adjutant General, Inspector General, Division Chaplain, Special Services Officer (including Graves Registration), Postal Officer, Finance Officer, Provost Marshal and when not with the Forward Echelon, the Military Government Officer and Chemical Officer, as well as attached speciality teams and Red Cross Field Directors.

There was, obviously, constant interchange between Forward and Rear Echelons, particularly between G-1 and G-4 section personnel. The Rear Echelon moved less frequently than the Forward and was billeted in more permanent shelter whenever practicable as was fitting to their duties.

THE INFANTRY DIVISION

The main feature of the World War II infantry division was its triangular organisation brought about by the elimination of the brigade level of command, the adaptation of the division to modern, open warfare and extensive use of motor transport. All these proposals had been urged by Gen Pershing back in the 1920s, but did not take on a solid shape until Gen Marshall took command. The new organisation comprised approximately 15,500 men as a 'general purpose organisation intended for open warfare in theatres permitting the use of motor transport'. They also had a minimum of artillery and other support elements organically assigned. Readjustments to the organisation in 1942 and 1943 constituted a shrinking process and not a complete reorganisation. Strength was reduced by about 8 per cent to 14,253. 2½ ton trucks regained preference over 1½ ton types and weapon changes included the replacement of the 37mm anti-tank gun by the 57mm. The 75mm howitzer was dropped and the towed 105mm howitzer took the place of the self-propelled type in the restored independent cannon company. The M1 (Garand) became the principal rifle, the bazooka was introduced in large numbers (557) and more jeeps with ¼ ton trailers were prescribed. An HQ special troops was formed to coordinate and supervise the activities of the division HQ company, military police platoon, ordnance light maintenance company,

Men of one of the D-Day assaulting infantry divisions wait to board their landing craft at Saltash, Devon, June 1944. GIs were festooned with kit, including the M-1926 US Navy lifebelt, which can be seen (deflated) around their waists – it looks like two tubes and was inflated with the mouth.

QM company and the signal company. Although quite well equipped with transport, there was not enough to lift the entire division and its equipment in one move, so extra transport had to be obtained from above.

Within the three infantry regiments the smallest sub-unit was the rifle squad of 12 men, armed with 10 M1 rifles, one Browning automatic rifle (BAR) and one M1903 Springfield sniper's rifle. Three squads made up a rifle platoon and three rifle platoons and one weapons platoon were grouped together to form a rifle company. The weapons platoon contained two .30cal light machine guns (LMG), three 60mm mortars, three bazookas and a .50cal heavy machine gun (HMG), primarily for AA defence. The total strength of a rifle company was 193 all ranks. A battalion comprised three such rifle companies, plus a heavy weapons company of six 81mm mortars, eight .30cal HMGs, seven bazookas and three .50cal HMGs. HQ company of the battalion held an anti-tank platoon of three 37mm/57mm anti-tank guns. Total battalion strength was 871 all ranks. An infantry regiment comprised three battalions, together with the following regimental units: HQ and HQ company; cannon company (six short-barrelled, towed 105mm); anti-tank company (12 x 37mm/57mm anti-tank guns and a mine laying platoon); and the service company which had the task of transporting supplies for the line battalions. Three infantry regiments made up the triangular division's total of 9,354 infantrymen.

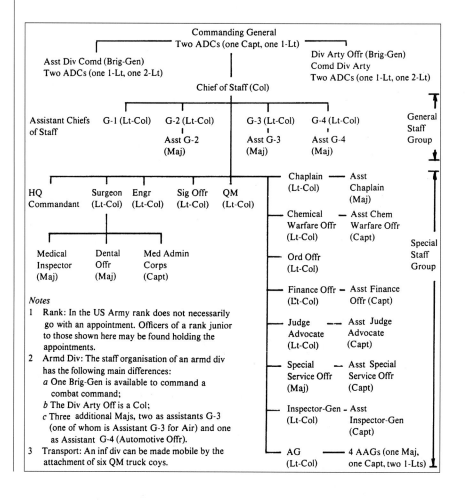

Fig 7 Staff of an Infantry Division HQ.

The field artillery in the division had an HQ and HQ battery, with three light artillery battalions and one medium artillery battalion under command. The former each comprised an HQ battery, service battery and three firing batteries of four 105mm towed howitzers. Medium artillery battalion had a similar organisation, with three firing batteries each of four towed 155mm howitzers. Total artillery manpower was 2,160. Auxiliary units included a reconnaissance troop, engineer battalion, medical battalion, QM company, ordnance company, signal company and a military police platoon. Together with all the attached personnel, such as unit medical sections and chaplains, the total strength was 14,253 all ranks. When large scale combat developed in 1944 the following units were normally attached: a mechanised cavalry squadron, one or more field artillery battalions of any appropriate calibre, chemical battalion (manning 4.2in mortars), tank, tank destroyer or anti-aircraft units. As a result an infantry divisional commander usually found himself commanding well over 15,000 men. There was no permanent combat command headquarters as with the armoured division. When combined arms teams were formed for independent missions then one of the three infantry regimental headquarters was used to command them and the group designated as a Combat Team, using the regimental number of the particular regiment (e.g. 385th CT).

THE ARMORED DIVISION

The role of the armoured division as stated in the *Armored Force Field Manual* (FM 17–10) of March 1942 was: 'the role of the armored force and its components in the conduct of highly mobile ground warfare is primarily offensive in character, by self-sustained units of great power and mobility composed of specially equipped troops of the required arms and services.' By January 1944 this had been simplified in the *Armored Division Manual* (FM 17–100) to read: 'The Armored division is organised primarily to perform missions that require great mobility and firepower.'

The original armoured division consisted of an armoured brigade of three tank regiments, two equipped with light tanks and one with mediums, plus a field artillery regiment of two battalions. There was also an armoured reconnaissance battalion and an attached air observation squadron for recce, while the support and service elements consisted of an armoured infantry regiment, a field artillery battalion, an engineer battalion, a signal company, a maintenance company, QM truck battalion and a medical battalion.

During World War II the armoured division underwent no fewer than six separate reorganisations; however, only two of these were really significant. The first, effective on 1 March 1942, resulted in what were called 'Heavy' armoured divisions. The armoured brigade organisation disappeared together with one of the armoured regiments, leaving in their place two combat commands (CCA and CCB) and two armoured regiments – see Table 1 Fig 9. There were three tank battalions in each regiment, but the proportion of light to medium tanks was altered, each

Organic Components of the Activated Infantry Division of World War II

Div	Inf Regts			Div Arty Fd Arty Bns				Special Troops Sig Coy	Ord Coy	QM Coy	Recce Tp	Engr Bn	Med Bn
1	16	18	26	5	7	32	33	1	701	1	1	1	1
2	9	23	38	12	15	37	38	2	702	2	2	2	2
3	7	15	30	9	10	39	41	3	703	3	3	10	3
4	8	12	22	20	29	42	44	4	704	4	4	4	4
5	2	10	11	19	21	46	50	5	705	5	5	7	5
6	1	20	63	1	51	53	80	6	706	6	6	6	6
7	17	32	184	31	48	49	57	7	707	7	7	13	7
8	13	28	121	28	43	45	56	8	708	8	8	12	8
9	39	47	60	26	34	60	84	9	709	9	9	15	9
10	85	86	87	604	605	616	-	110	710	10	10	126	10
24	19	21	34	11	13	52	63	24	724	24	24	3	24
25	27	35	161	8	64	89	90	25	725	25	25	65	25
26	101	104	328	101	102	180	263	39	726	26	26	101	114
27	105	106	165	104	105	106	249	27	727	27	27	102	102
28	109	110	112	107	108	109	229	28	728	28	28	103	103
29	115	116	175	110	111	224	227	29	729	29	29	121	104
30	117	119	120	113	118	197	230	30	730	30	30	105	105
31	124	155	167	114	116	117	149	31	731	31	31	106	106
32	126	127	128	120	121	126	129	32	732	32	32	114	107
33	123	130	136	122	123	124	210	33	733	33	33	108	108
34	133	135	168	125	151	175	185	34	734	34	34	109	109
35	134	137	320	127	161	216	219	35	735	35	35	60	110
36	141	142	143	131	132	133	155	36	736	36	36	111	111
37	129	145	148	6	135	136	140	37	737	37	37	117	112
38	149	151	152	138	139	150	163	38	738	38	38	113	113
40	108	160	185	143	164	213	222	40	740	40	40	115	115
41	162	163	186	146	167	205	218	41	741	41	41	116	116
42	222	232	242	232	292	402	542	132	742	42	42	142	122
43	103	169	172	103	152	169	192	43	743	43	43	118	118
44	71	114	324	156	157	217	220	44	744	44	44	63	119
45	157	179	180	158	160	171	189	45	700	45	45	120	120
63	253	254	255	718	861	862	863	563	763	63	63	263	363
65	259	260	261	720	867	868	869	556	765	65	65	265	365
66	262	263	264	721	870	871	872	566	766	66	66	266	366
69	271	272	273	724	879	880	881	569	769	69	69	269	369
70	274	275	276	725	882	883	884	570	770	70	70	270	370
71	5	14	66	564	607	608	609	571	771	251	71	271	371
75	289	290	291	730	897	898	899	575	775	75	75	275	375
76	304	385	417	302	355	364	901	76	776	76	76	301	301
77	305	306	307	304	305	306	902	77	777	77	77	302	302
78	309	310	311	307	308	309	903	78	778	78	78	303	303
79	313	314	315	310	311	312	904	79	779	79	79	304	304
80	317	318	319	313	314	315	905	80	780	80	80	305	305
81	321	322	323	316	317	318	906	81	781	81	81	306	306
83	329	330	331	322	323	324	908	83	783	83	83	308	308
84	333	334	335	325	326	327	909	84	784	84	84	309	309
85	337	338	339	328	329	403	910	85	785	85	85	310	310
86	341	342	343	331	332	404	911	86	786	86	86	311	311
87	345	346	347	334	335	336	912	87	787	87	87	312	312
88	349	350	351	337	338	339	913	88	788	88	88	313	313
89	353	354	355	340	341	563	914	89	714	405	89	314	314
90	357	358	359	343	344	345	915	90	790	90	90	315	315
91	361	362	363	346	347	348	916	91	791	91	91	316	316
92	365	370	371	597	598	599	600	92	792	92	92	317	317
93	25	368	369	593	594	595	596	93	793	93	93	318	318
94	301	302	376	301	356	390	919	94	794	94	94	319	319
95	377	378	379	358	359	360	920	95	795	95	95	320	320
96	381	382	383	361	362	363	921	96	796	96	96	321	321
97	303	386	387	303	386	389	922	97	797	97	97	322	322
98	389	390	391	367	368	399	923	98	798	98	98	323	323
99	393	394	395	370	371	372	924	99	799	99	99	324	324
100	397	398	399	373	374	375	925	100	800	100	100	325	325
102	405	406	407	379	380	381	927	102	802	102	102	327	327
103	409	410	411	382	383	384	928	103	803	103	103	328	328
104	413	414	415	385	386	387	929	104	804	104	104	329	329
106	422	423	424	589	590	591	592	106	806	106	106	81	331
American	132	164	182	245	246	247	221	26	721	125	21	57	121

A comparison of Strengths and Principal Weapons of the Infantry Division
1941/42/43/45

	T/O 7 and allied tables as changed to 1 June 1941	T/O 7 and allied tables 1 Aug 1942	T/O & E 7 and allied tables 15 July 1943	T/O & E 7 and allied tables 24 Jan 1945
Entire Div	15,245	15,514	14,253	14,037
Div HQ	102	169	158	166
INFANTRY	10,020	9,999	9,354	9,204
Inf Regt (3)	3,340	3,333	3,118	3,068
HQ & HQ Coy	178	132	108	104
Service Coy	152	132	114	111
ATk Coy	185	169	165	159
Cannon Coy	–	123	118	114
Band	29	29	–	–
Inf Bn (3)	932	916	871	860
HQ & HQ Coy	52	139	126	121
Heavy Weapons Coy	211	183	166	160
Rifle Coy (3)	223	198	193	193
FIELD ARTILLERY	2,685	2,479	2,160	2,111
HQ & HQ Bty Div Arty	119	116	114	114
Band	29	28	–	–
Lt Arty Bn (3)	584	576	509	497
HQ Bty	142	165	132	126
Service Bty	82	78	77	74
Firing Bty (3)	120	111	100	99
Med Arty Bn	785	607	519	506
HQ Bty	142	158	115	112
Service Bty	95	89	77	76
Firing Bty (3)	134	120	109	106
ATk Bty	146	–	–	–
AUXILIARY UNITS	2,004	2,340	2,074	2,046
Recce Tp	147	201	155	149
Engr Bn	634	745	647	620
Med Bn	520	504	465	443
QM Coy	312	344	193	186
Ord Coy	–	–	147	141
Sig Coy	261	322	226	239
MP Pl	67	80	73	106
Div HQ Coy	63	144	110	104
Band	–	–	58	58
ATTACHED MEDICAL	423	515	494	497
Inf Regt (3)	106	136	135	136
Div Arty	83	76	57	57
Engr Bn	14	23	17	17
QM	8	8	–	–
Special Troops	–	–	15	15
Attached Chaplain	11	12	13	13
Principal Armament				
Rifles .30cal	6,942	6,233	6,518	6,349
Auto Rifles .30cal	375	567	243	405
MGs .30cal	179	147	157	211
MGs .50cal	113	133	236	237
Mortars 60mm	81	81	90	90
Mortars 81mm	36	57	54	54
ATk Rocket Launchers	–	–	557	558
ATk guns 37mm	60	109	–	–
ATk guns 57mm	–	–	57	57
Guns 75mm	8	–	–	–
Hows 75mm SP	–	18	–	–
Hows 105mm	36	36	54	54
Hows 105mm SP	–	6	–	–
Hows 155mm	12	12	12	12
Vehicles All Types (except boats and a/c)	1,834	2,149	2,012	2,114

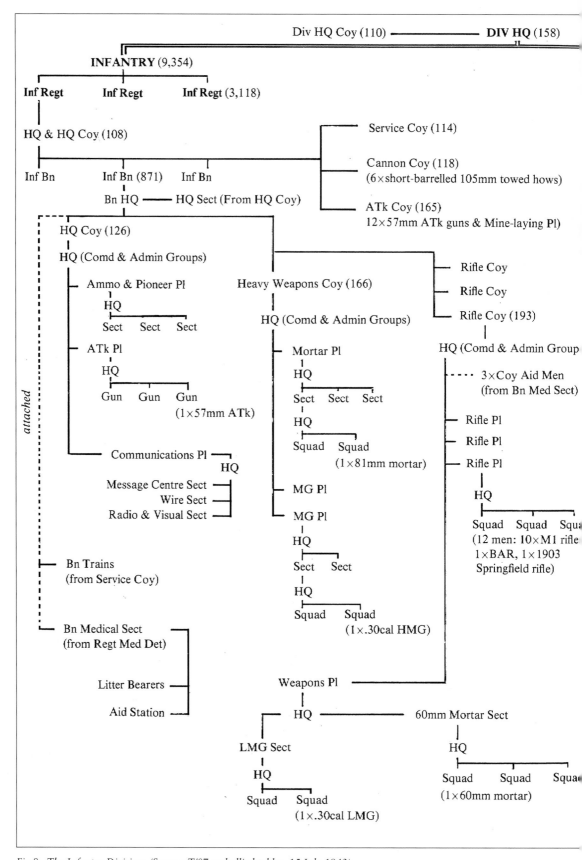

Fig 8   The Infantry Division. (Source: T/07 and allied tables, 15 July 1943)

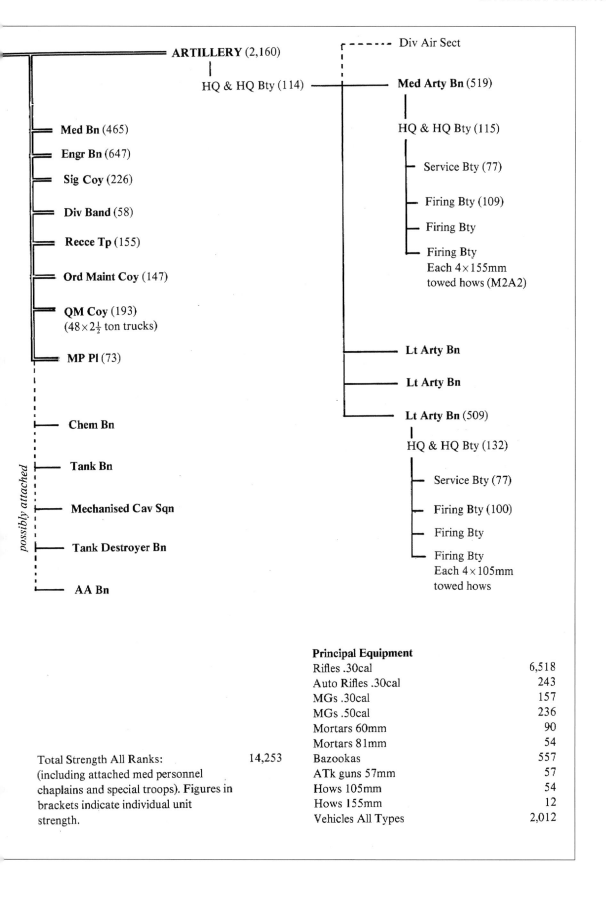

ARTILLERY (2,160)

Div Air Sect

HQ & HQ Bty (114)

Med Arty Bn (519)

HQ & HQ Bty (115)

Service Bty (77)

Firing Bty (109)

Firing Bty

Firing Bty
Each 4×155mm
towed hows (M2A2)

Med Bn (465)

Engr Bn (647)

Sig Coy (226)

Div Band (58)

Recce Tp (155)

Ord Maint Coy (147)

QM Coy (193)
(48×2½ ton trucks)

MP Pl (73)

Lt Arty Bn

Lt Arty Bn

Lt Arty Bn (509)

HQ & HQ Bty (132)

Service Bty (77)

Firing Bty (100)

Firing Bty

Firing Bty
Each 4×105mm
towed hows

possibly attached

Chem Bn

Tank Bn

Mechanised Cav Sqn

Tank Destroyer Bn

AA Bn

Principal Equipment

Rifles .30cal	6,518
Auto Rifles .30cal	243
MGs .30cal	157
MGs .50cal	236
Mortars 60mm	90
Mortars 81mm	54
Bazookas	557
ATk guns 57mm	57
Hows 105mm	54
Hows 155mm	12
Vehicles All Types	2,012

Total Strength All Ranks: 14,253
(including attached med personnel
chaplains and special troops). Figures in
brackets indicate individual unit
strength.

Tank crewmen of a US armoured division check their equipment in a marshalling area in the UK, prior to loading for Normandy.

regiment having two medium and one light battalion. Artillery was also reorganised into three separate battalions. The combat commands gave the division more flexibility, as their composition could be varied to fit with the divisional commander's assessment of the battle situation.

The second major reorganisation, effective 15 September 1943 (see Table 2 Fig 9), produced what was called the 'light' armoured division. It reduced the tank strength by replacing the two regiments (i.e. six tank battalions) by three tank battalions. The regimental organisation was abolished in all armoured divisions except for the 2nd and 3rd which remained on the old organisation. This should have meant that the tank strength of the division was halved (three instead of six battalions); in fact, as the table shows, the actual reduction was about one-third. Another combat command was introduced to control the division reserves, known as CCR (or CCC). A cavalry recce squadron replaced the recce battalion and the total divisional strength fell by nearly 4,000. The 1943 reorganisation took time to effect; for example, 1st Armored in Italy did not change until July 1944.

In summary, it can be said that the various organisations followed four trends: increasing the infantry element; eliminating unnecessary levels of command; slimming down the service support elements and increasing the medium tanks at the expense of light tanks. By 1945 yet another type of armoured division had been proposed, based upon the

Table 1: Armoured Division, T/O 17 of 1 March 1942

Entire Div	14,620	LMGs .30cal	237
Div HQ	307	LMGs (ground) .30cal	54
HQ Coy	111	MGs HB .50cal	103
Service Coy	160	SMGs (inc on ord vehicles)	1,654
Armd Sig Coy	256	SMGs (on ¼ ton trucks)	506
Armd Recce Bn	872	Mortars 60mm	57
Armd Regts (2)	2,424	Mortars 81mm	27
Armd Field Arty Bns (3)	709	ATk Guns SP	126
Armd Inf Regt	2,389	ATk Guns Towed	68
Armd Engr Bn	1,174	Hows 105mm SP	54
Div Trains	1,948	Assault Guns SP	42
Attached Medical	414	Lt Tanks (w/armament)	158
Attached Chaplain	14	Med Tanks (w/armament)	232
		Armd Cars Recce (w/armament)	79
Principal Armament		M2 Halftracks (w/armament)	691
Rifles .30cal	1,628	M3 Halftracks (w/o/armament)	42
Carbines .30cal	6,042	Scout Car (w/armament)	40
Pistols .45cal	3,850	Other Vehicles (inc trailers)	2,146

Table 2: Armoured Division, T/O 17 of 14 September 1943

Entire Div	10,937	*Principal Armament*	
Div HQ	164	Rifles .30cal	2,063
Tank Bns (3)	729	Carbines .30cal	5,286
Inf Bns (3)	1,001	MGs .30cal	465
CC HQ & HQ Coy (2)	184	MGs .50cal	404
Div Trains HQ & HQ Coy	103	Mortars 60mm	63
CCR HQ	8	Mortars 81mm	30
Field Arty	1,623	ATk Rocket Launchers	607
Auxiliary Units:		Hows 57mm	30
Cav Recce Sqn (Mechanised)	935	Hows 75mm	17
Engr Bn	693	Hows 105mm	54
Med Bn	417	Med Tanks	186
Ord Bn	762	Lt Tanks	77
Sig Coy	302	Armd Cars	54
MP Pl	91	Halftracks carriers	455
Div HQ Coy	138	Halftracks 81mm Mortar Carriers	18
Band	58	Vehicles All Types (except boats & a/c)	2,650
Attached Medical	261	Less Combat Types	1,761
Attached Chaplain	8		

Table 3: Armoured Division, T/O 17 of 16 June 1945

Entire Div	10,670	*Principal Armament*	
Div HQ	174	Rifles .30cal	1,980
Tank Bns (3)	700	Carbines .30cal	4,998
Inf Bns (3)	995	Auto Rifles .30cal	81
Recce Sqn	894	MGs .30cal	433
Field Arty	1,625	MGs .50cal	385
Auxiliary Units:		Mortars 60mm	27
CC HQ & HQ Coy (2)	178	Mortars 81mm	12
Engr Bn	660	ATk Rocket Launchers	609
Div Trains HQ & HQ Coy	99	ATk Guns 57mm	30
Med Bn	400	Lt Tanks	77
Ord Bn	732	Med Tanks	168
Sig Coy	293	Med Tanks (105mm how)	27
MP Pl	87	Armd Cars	50
Div HQ Coy	115	Halftracks	452
CCR HQ	8	Motor Carriages 75mm	8
Band	58	Motor Carriages 105mm	54
Attached Medical	254	Halftracks Mortar Carriers	18
Attached Chaplain	8	Vehicles All Types (except boats & a/c)	1,869

Fig 9 A Comparison of the Organisations of the Armoured Division 1942/43/45.

experience of armoured commanders, namely for a heavy type division with the capability of performing missions well outside the capabilities of the 'light' armoured division. As this new 'heavy' division organisation did not become effective until 1948, I have not included any details apart from Table 3 Fig 9.

ORGANISATIONAL TABLES

The organisation shown in Figs 10–23 is based upon the 1943 organisation and thus shows the 'light' division as this is the one which fought the most battles. It had five commands under divisional control – CCA, CCB, CCR, Artillery Command and Trains Command. Each HQ had an HQ company or detachment. Each was designed to control whatever subordinate units were assigned to it for a particular mission. The major units of the division were the tank battalions, each comprising an HQ and HQ company, three medium tank companies, one light tank company and a service company. Total manpower of a tank battalion was 729. Each tank company contained 17 tanks, with three platoons of five and two in company HQ. Towards the end of the war, an extra M4 medium tank, mounting a 105mm howitzer was added to company HQ, increasing the medium tank strength of the division to 195. Balancing the three tank battalions were three armoured infantry battalions, each composed of an HQ and HQ company, a service company and three rifle companies. Total battalion manpower was 1,001. In support were three armoured artillery battalions each of 18 105mm self-propelled howitzers (M7).

Organic Components of the Activated Armoured Division of World War II

Div	Armd Inf Bns			Tk Bns			Div Arty	Armd Arty	Armd Fd Bns	Cav Recce Sqn	Armd Eng Bn	Armd Med Bn	Armd Ord Bn	Armd Sig Coy	Combat Commands
1	6	11	14	1	4	13	27	68	91	81	16	47	123	141	A –B – R
2								14	78	92	82	17	48	2	142	A – B – R
3								54	67	391	83	23	45	3	143	A – B – R
4	10	51	53	8	35	37	22	66	94	25	24	4	126	144	A – B – R
5	15	46	47	10	34	81	47	71	95	85	22	75	127	145	A – B – R
6	9	44	50	15	68	69	128	212	231	86	25	76	128	146	A – B – R
7	23	38	48	17	31	40	434	440	489	87	33	77	129	147	A – B – R
8	7	49	58	18	36	80	398	399	405	88	53	78	130	148	A – B – R
9	27	52	60	2	14	19	3	16	73	89	9	2	131	149	A – B – R
10	20	54	61	3	11	21	419	420	423	90	55	80	132	150	A – B – R
11	21	55	63	22	41	42	490	491	492	41	56	81	133	151	A – B – R
12	17	56	66	23	43	714	493	494	495	92	119	82	134	152	A – B – R
13	16	59	67	24	45	46	496	497	498	93	124	83	135	153	A – B – R
14	19	62	68	25	47	48	499	500	501	94	125	84	136	154	A – B – R
16	18	64	69	5	16	26	393	396	397	23	216	216	137	156	A – B – R
20	8	65	70	9	20	27	412	413	414	30	220	220	138	160	A – B – R

Note: 2d and 3d Armd Divs remained as 'heavy' divisions throughout the war with two armd regts and one armd inf regt each. These were numbered: 2d Armd Div: 41st Armd Inf Regt, 66th and 67th Armd Regts. 3rd Armd Div: 36th Armd Inf Regt, 32d and 33d Armd Regts.

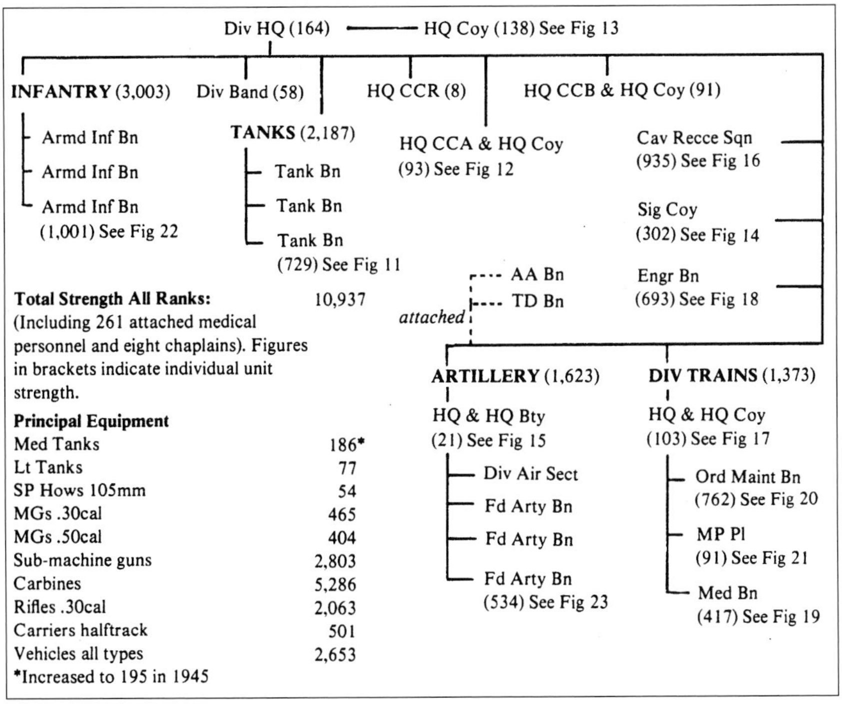

Total Strength All Ranks: 10,937
(Including 261 attached medical personnel and eight chaplains). Figures in brackets indicate individual unit strength.

Principal Equipment

Med Tanks	186*
Lt Tanks	77
SP Hows 105mm	54
MGs .30cal	465
MGs .50cal	404
Sub-machine guns	2,803
Carbines	5,286
Rifles .30cal	2,063
Carriers halftrack	501
Vehicles all types	2,653

*Increased to 195 in 1945

Fig 10 Armoured Division. (Source: T/017 and allied tables from 15 September 1943)

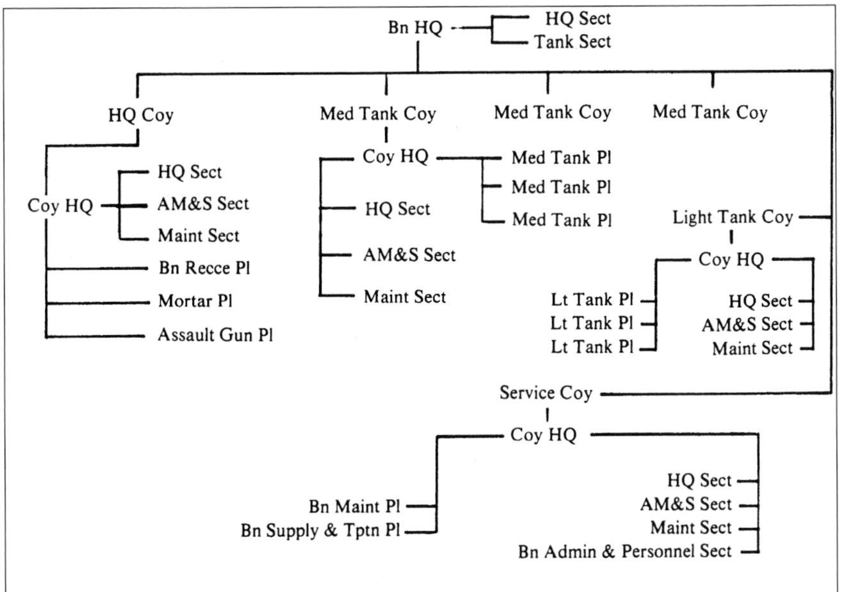

Bn HQ: HQ Sect 4×¼ ton trucks, 2×M3 halftracks; Tank Sect 2×M4 tanks.
HQ Coy: *Coy HQ:* HQ Sect 1×¼ ton truck, 1×M3 halftrack; AM&S Sect 1×2½ ton truck, 1×1 ton trailer; Maint Sect 1×¼ ton truck, 1×M3 halftrack. *Bn Recce Pl* 5×¼ ton trucks, 1×M3 halftrack. *Mortar Pl* 1×M3 halftrack, 3×M21 81mm mortar carriers. *Assault Gun Pl* 2×M3 halftracks, 3×M4 tanks (105mm hows), 4×M10 ammo carriers.
Med Tank Coy: *Coy HQ:* HQ Sect 1×¼ ton truck, 2×M4 tanks, 1×M4 (105mm how); AM&S Sect 1×2½ ton truck, 1×1 ton trailer; Maint Sect 1×¼ ton truck, 1×M3 halftrack, 1×M32 ARV. Three *Tank Pls* each of 5×M4 med tanks.
Lt Tank Coy: *Coy HQ:* HQ Sect 1×¼ ton truck, 2×M5 lt tanks; AM&S Sect 1×2½ ton truck, 1×1 ton trailer; Maint Sect 1×¼ ton truck, 1×M3 halftrack, 1×lt ARV. Three *Tank Pls* each of 5×M5 lt tanks.
Service Coy: *Coy HQ:* HQ Sect 1×¾ ton truck; AM&S Sect 1×2½ ton truck, 1×1 ton trailer; Maint Sect 1×¼ ton truck, 1×2½ ton truck, 1×1 ton trailer; Bn Admin & Personnel Sect 1×2½ ton truck, 1×1 ton trailer. *Bn Maint Pl* 1×¼ ton truck, 1×¾ ton truck, 2×2½ ton trucks, 2×1 ton trailer, 2×M32 ARV, 2×heavy wreckers. *Bn Supply & Tptn Pl* 1×¼ ton truck, 1×¾ ton truck, 29×2½ ton trucks, 15×1 ton trailers, 13×M10 ammo trailers.

Fig 11 Tank Battalion.

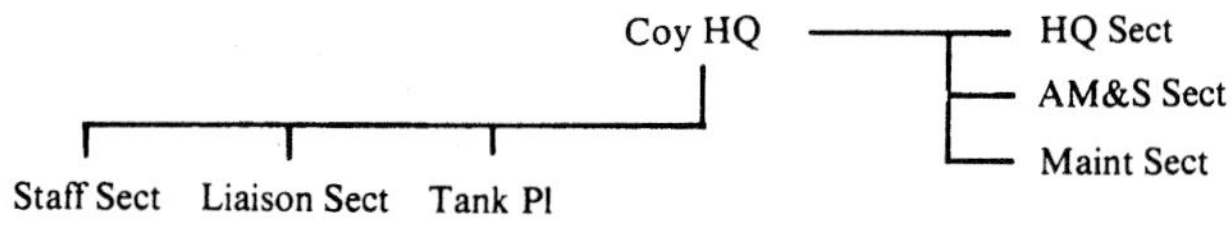

HQ Coy: *Coy HQ:* HQ Sect 1×M3 halftrack; AM&S Sect 2×2½ ton trucks, 1×1 ton trailer, 1×M10 ammo trailer; Maint Sect 1×M3 halftrack, 1×1 ton trailer. *Staff Section* 3×¼ ton trucks, 2×¼ ton trailers, 5×M3 halftracks. *Liaison Sect* 5×¼ ton trucks. *Tank Pl* 3×M5 lt tanks.

Fig 12 Combat Command HQ & HQ Company. (CAA, CCB, CCR)

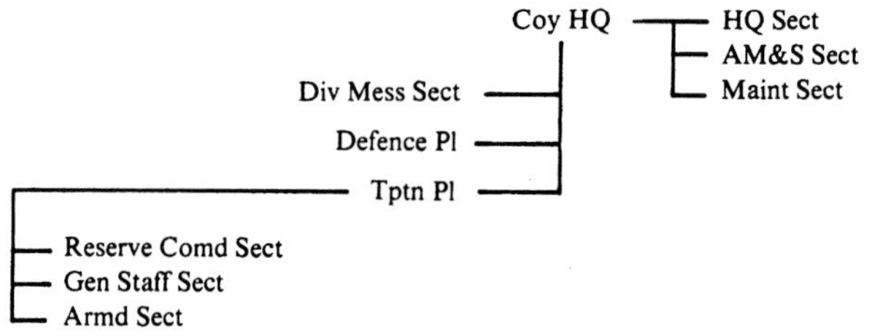

HQ Coy: *Coy HQ:* HQ Sect 1×¼ ton truck, 1×M3 halftrack; AM&S Sect 1×¾ ton truck, 1×2½ ton truck, 1×1 ton trailer; Maint Sect 1×¼ ton truck, 1×¾ ton truck, 1×2½ ton truck, 1×1 ton trailer; Div Mess Sect 1×2½ ton truck, 1×1 ton trailer. *Defence Pl* 1×¼ ton truck, 3×M3 halftracks each with 1×57mm ATk gun. *Tptn Pl:* HQ Sect 1×¼ ton truck; Res Comd Sect 1×¼ ton truck, 2×M3 halftracks; Gen Staff Sect 5×¼ ton trucks, 6×M3 halftracks; Armd Sect 2×M8 armd cars, 3×M5 lt tanks.

Fig 13 Division HQ Company.

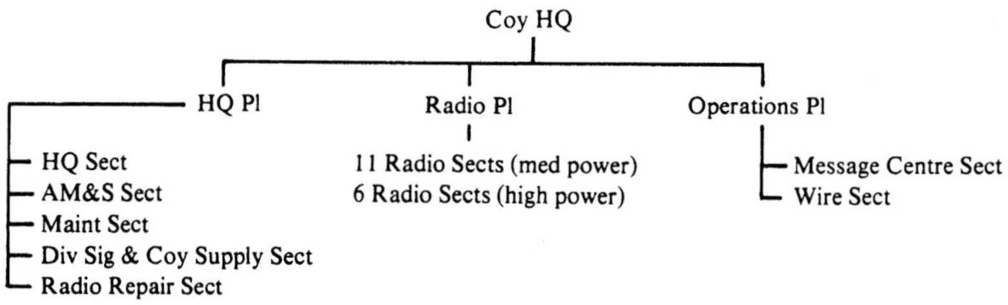

HQ Pl: HQ Sect 1×¼ ton truck, 1×M3 halftrack; AM&S Sect 2×2½ ton trucks, 2×1 ton trailers; Maint Sect 1×¼ ton truck, 1×M3 halftrack, 2×2½ ton trucks, 2×1 ton trailers; Div Sig & Coy Supply Sect 2×¼ ton trucks, 1×¼ ton trailer, 4×2½ ton trucks, 4×1 ton trailers; Radio Repair Sect 2×M3 halftracks, 2×2½ ton sig repair trucks, 2×2½ ton trucks, 2×1 ton trailers. *Ops Pl:* Message Centre Sect 14×¼ ton trucks, 2×M3 halftracks; Wire Sect 5×¼ ton trucks, 2×M3 halftracks, 3×2½ ton trucks. *Radio Pl:* 11 Radio Sect med power each 1×M3 halftrack; Six Radio Sects high power each 1×2½ ton radio trucks, 1×K52 signal trailers.

Fig 14 Armoured Signal Company.

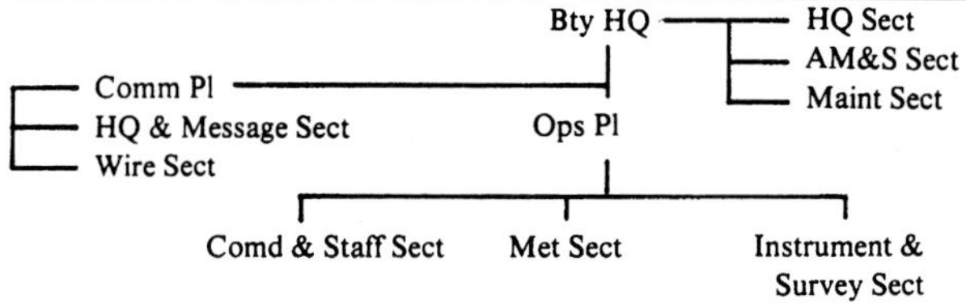

HQ Bty: *Bty HQ:* HQ Sect 2×¼ ton trucks, 1×¼ ton trailer; AM&S Sect 1×2½ ton truck, 1×1 ton trailer; Maint Sect 1×¼ ton truck, 1×¼ ton trailer, 1×¾ ton truck, 1×2½ ton truck, 1×1 ton trailer. *Comm Pl:* Wire Sect 2×¾ ton trucks, 1×2½ ton truck; HQ & Message Sect 3×¼ ton trucks, 1×¾ ton truck. *Operations Pl:* Met Sect 1×2½ ton truck, 1×1 ton trailer; Instrument & Survey Sect 1×¼ ton truck, 1×¾ ton truck; Comd & Staff Sect 3×¾ ton trucks, 1×M8 armd car, 1×2½ ton truck, 1×1 ton trailer, 2×liaison aeroplanes.

Fig 15 Division Artillery HQ Battery.

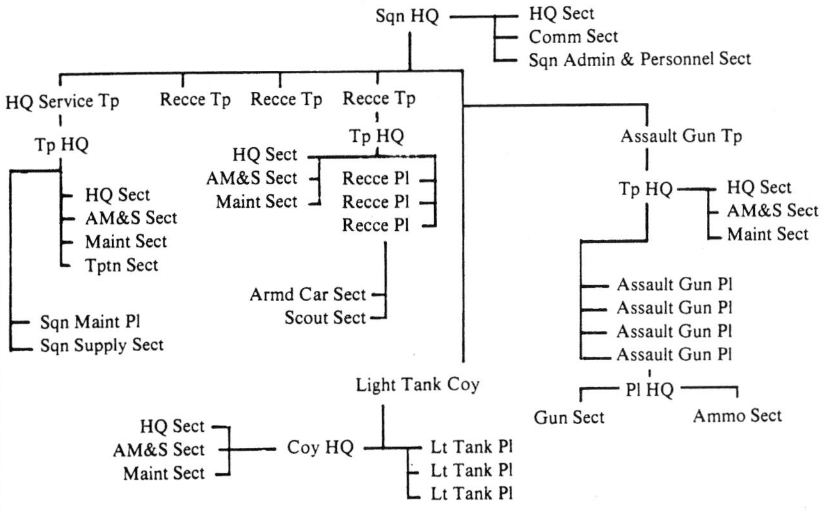

HQ & HQ Service Tp: *Sqn HQ:* HQ Sect 2×¼ ton trucks, 2×M3 halftracks; Comm Sect 4×¼ ton trucks, 3×M8 armd cars, 1×M3 halftrack; Sqn Admin & Personnel Sect 1×¼ ton truck, 1×2½ ton truck, 1×1 ton trailer.
HQ Service Tp: *TP HQ:* HQ Sect 1×¼ ton truck; AM&S Sect 1×2½ ton truck, 1×1 ton trailer; Maint Sect 1×M3 halftrack, 1×1 ton trailer; Tptn Sect 1×¼ ton truck, 6×2½ ton trucks, 4×1 ton trailers, 2×M10 ammo trailers. *Sqn Maint Pl* 1×¼ ton truck, 1×M8 armd car, 1×M32 ARV, 1×M3 halftrack, 1×6 ton heavy wrecker, 2×2½ ton trucks, 2×1 ton trailers. *Sqn Supply Sect* 3×2½ ton trucks, 3×1 ton trailers.
Recce Tps: *Tp HQ:* HQ Sect 3×¼ ton trucks, 2×M8 armd cars; AM&S Sect 3×M3 halftracks, 1×2½ ton truck, 4×1 ton trailers; Maint Sect 1×¼ ton truck, 1×M8 armd car, 1×M3 halftrack, 1×1 ton trailer. Three *Recce Pls* each of: Armd Car Sect 3×M8 armd cars; Scout Sect 6×¼ ton trucks.
Assault Gun Tp: *Tp HQ:* HQ Sect 1×¼ ton truck, 1×M3 halftrack; AM&S Sect 1×2½ ton truck, 1×1 ton trailer; Maint Sect 1×¼ ton truck, 1×M3 halftrack, 1×lt ARV. Four *Assault Gun Pls of:* Pl HQ 1×M3 halftrack; Ammo Sect 1×M3 halftrack, 1×M10 ammo trailer; Gun Sect 2×M8 75mm carriage hows, 2×M10 ammo trailers.
Lt Tank Coy: *Coy HQ:* HQ Sect 1×¼ ton truck, 2×M5 lt tanks; AM&S Sect 1×2½ ton truck, 1×1 ton trailer; Maint Sect 1×¼ ton truck, 1×M3 halftrack, 1×lt ARV. Three *Lt Tank Pls* of: 5×M5 lt tanks.

Fig 16 Cavalry Recce Squadron.

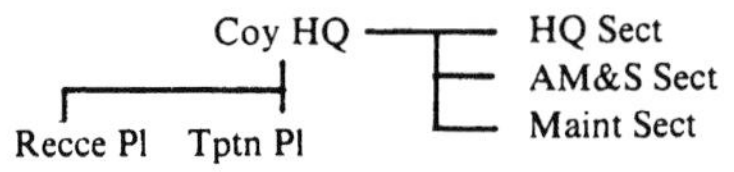

HQ Coy: *Coy HQ:* HQ Sect 2×¼ ton trucks; AM&S Sect 1×¾ ton truck, 2×2½ ton trucks, 2×1 ton trailers; Maint Sect 1×¼ ton truck, 1×¾ ton truck, 1×2½ ton truck, 1×1 ton trailer. *Recce Pl:* 4×¼ ton trucks. *Tptn Pl:* 1×5 passenger car, 5×¼ ton trucks, 8×¾ ton trucks, 6×2½ ton trucks, 6×1 ton trailers.

Fig 17 Division Trains HQ Company.

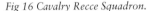

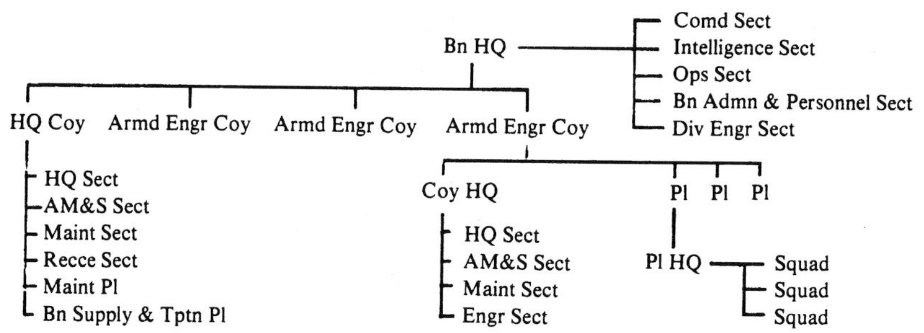

HQ & HQ Coy: *Bn HQ:* Comd Sect 1×¼ ton truck, 3×M3 halftracks; Intelligence Sect 1×¼ ton truck; Ops Sect 1×¾ ton truck; Div Engr Sect 1×¾ ton truck; Bn Admin & Personnel Sect 1×2½ ton truck, 1×1 ton trailer.

HQ Coy: *Coy HQ:* HQ Sect 1×¼ ton truck; AM&S Sect 1×2½ ton truck, 1×1 ton trailer; Maint Sect 1×¼ ton truck, 1×¾ ton truck; Recce Sect 4×¼ ton trucks. *Maint Pl* 1×¼ ton truck, 1×¾ ton truck, 1×6 ton heavy wrecker, 1×motorised shop, 1×welding equipment trailer, 2×2½ ton trucks, 1×1 ton trailer. *Bn Supply & Tptn Pl* 1×¼ ton truck, 1×truck mounted compressor, 3×3 ton bridge trucks, 4×water equipment trailers, 11×2½ ton trucks, 9×1 ton trailers, 2×M10 ammo trailers.

Armd Engr Coy: *Coy HQ:* HQ Sect 1×¼ ton truck, 1×M3 halftrack; AM&S Sect 1×2½ ton truck, 1×1 ton trailer; Maint Sect 1×¼ ton truck, 1×¾ ton truck; Engr Sect 1×truck mounted compressor, 1×65dbhp tractor (bulldozer), 1×20 ton semi-trailer and tractor, 1×6 ton bridge truck. *1 Pl:* Pl HQ 1×¼ ton truck, 1×2½ ton cargo truck, 1×1 ton trailer, 1×2½ ton utility trailer pulled by squad M3; three Squads each with 1×M3 halftrack. *2 & 3 Pl:* Pl HQ 1×¼ ton truck, 1×2½ ton cargo truck, 1×1 ton trailer, 1×2½ ton utility trailer pulled by squad truck; three Squads each with 1×2½ ton dump truck.

Fig 18 Armoured Engineer Battalion.

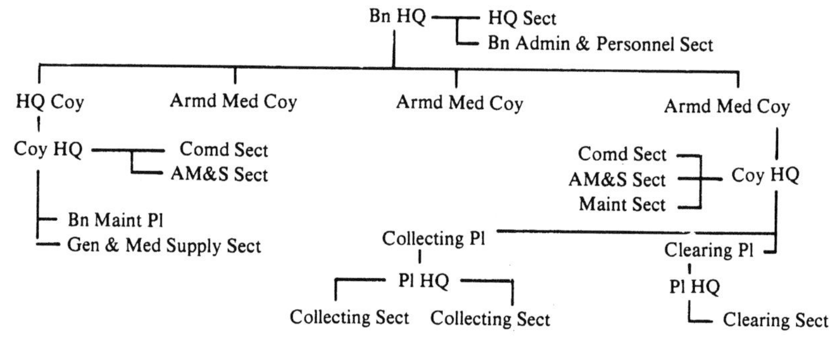

Bn HQ: HQ Sect 2×¼ ton trucks, 1×¾ ton truck, 1×M3 halftrack; Bn Admin & Personnel Sect 1×¾ ton truck.

HQ Coy: *Coy HQ:* Comd Sect 1×¾ ton truck; AM&S Sect 1×2½ ton truck, 1×1 ton trailer; *Bn Maint Pl* 1×¼ ton truck, 2×2½ ton trucks, 2×1 ton trailer; *Gen & Med Supply Sect* 1×¼ ton truck, 5×2½ ton trucks, 5×1 ton trailers.

Armd Med Coy: *Coy HQ:* Comd Sect 1×¼ ton truck, 1×M3 halftrack; AM&S Sect 1×2½ ton truck, 1×1 ton trailer; Maint Sect 1×¾ ton truck. *Collecting Pl:* Pl HQ 1×¼ ton truck, 1×¾ ton truck, 1st Collecting Sect 5×¾ ton ambulances; 2nd Collecting Sect 5×¾ ton ambulances. *Clearing Pl:* Pl HQ 1×¾ ton truck; Clearing Sect 1×¾ ton truck, 2×2½ ton trucks, 2×2½ ton surgical trucks, 2×1 ton trailers, 2×250gal water trailers.

Fig 19 Armoured Medical Battalion.

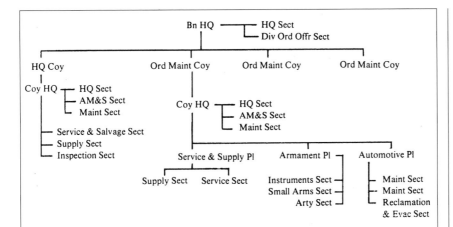

Bn HQ: Div Ord Offr Sect $1\times\frac{1}{4}$ ton truck, $1\times\frac{3}{4}$ ton truck, $1\times2\frac{1}{2}$ ton truck, 1×1 ton trailer; HQ Sect $3\times\frac{1}{4}$ ton trucks, $1\times\frac{3}{4}$ ton truck, $1\times$M3 halftrack, $2\times2\frac{1}{2}$ ton trucks, 1×1 ton trailer.

HQ Coy: *Coy HQ:* HQ Sect $1\times\frac{3}{4}$ ton truck; AM&S Sect $1\times2\frac{1}{2}$ ton truck, 1×1 ton trailer; Maint Sect $1\times\frac{1}{4}$ ton truck, $1\times\frac{3}{4}$ ton truck. *Service & Salvage Sect* 2×6 ton heavy wreckers, $2\times2\frac{1}{2}$ ton machine shop trucks, $3\times2\frac{1}{2}$ ton trucks. *Inspection Sect* $3\times\frac{1}{4}$ ton trucks, $1\times2\frac{1}{2}$ ton truck. *Supply Sect* $26\times2\frac{1}{2}$ ton trucks, 26×1 ton trailers.

Ord Maint Coy: *Coy HQ:* HQ Sect $1\times\frac{1}{4}$ ton truck, $1\times$M3 halftrack; AM&S Sect $1\times2\frac{1}{2}$ ton truck, 1×1 ton trailer; Maint Sect $1\times\frac{1}{4}$ ton truck. *Service & Supply Pl:* Service Sect $1\times\frac{1}{4}$ ton truck, $1\times2\frac{1}{2}$ ton truck, $1\times2\frac{1}{2}$ ton machine shop truck; Supply Sect $6\times2\frac{1}{2}$ ton trucks, 6×1 ton trailers. *Armament Pl:* Arty Sect $1\times\frac{1}{4}$ ton truck, $1\times2\frac{1}{2}$ ton arty repair truck, $1\times2\frac{1}{2}$ ton truck, 1×1 ton trailer; Small Arms Sect $1\times\frac{1}{4}$ ton truck, $1\times2\frac{1}{2}$ ton small arms repair truck; Instrument Sect $1\times\frac{1}{4}$ ton truck, $1\times2\frac{1}{2}$ ton instrument repair truck. *Automotive Pl:* Pl HQ $2\times\frac{1}{4}$ ton trucks, $1\times\frac{3}{4}$ ton truck, $4\times2\frac{1}{2}$ ton trucks, 4×1 ton trailers, $1\times2\frac{1}{2}$ ton decontamination truck, $1\times2\frac{1}{2}$ ton electrical repair truck, 1×6 ton heavy wrecker; two Maint Sects each with $1\times\frac{1}{4}$ ton truck, $1\times2\frac{1}{2}$ ton truck, 1×1 ton trailer; Reclamation and Evac Sect 2×6 ton heavy wreckers, $1\times2\frac{1}{2}$ ton truck, 1×1 ton trailer, $3\times$transporter tractor trucks, $3\times$transporter semi-trailers.

Fig 20 Ordnance Maintenance Battalion.

Pl HQ $1\times\frac{1}{4}$ ton truck, $1\times\frac{3}{4}$ ton truck, $1\times$M3 halftrack. *Police Sect* $1\times\frac{1}{4}$ ton truck, $2\times\frac{3}{4}$ ton trucks. *Traffic Sect:* HQ Sect $1\times\frac{1}{4}$ ton truck; four Squads each with $4\times\frac{1}{4}$ ton trucks.

Fig 21 MP Platoon

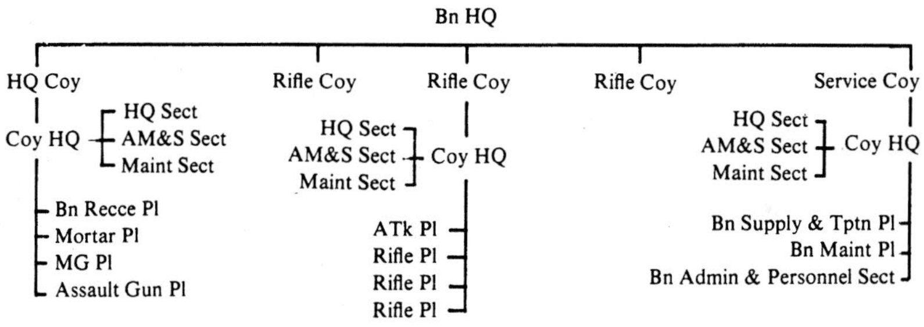

Bn HQ 4×¼ ton trucks, 2×M3 halftracks.
HQ Coy: *Coy HQ:* HQ Sect 1×¼ ton truck, 1×M3 halftrack; AM&S Sect 1×2½ ton truck, 1×1 ton trailer; Maint Sect 1×¼ ton truck, 1×M3 halftrack, 1×1 ton trailer. *Bn Recce Pl* 5×¼ ton trucks, 1×M3 halftrack. *Mortar Pl* 1×M3 halftrack, 3×M21 81mm mortar carriers. *MG Pl* 3×M3 halftracks. *Assault Gun Pl* 2×M3 halftracks, 3×M7 105mm hows, 4×M10 ammo trailers.
Rifle Coy: *Coy HQ:* HQ Sect 1×¼ ton truck, 1×M3 halftrack; AM&S Sect 2×2½ ton trucks, 2×1 ton trailers; Maint Sect 1×¼ ton truck, 1×M3 halftrack, 1×1 ton trailer. *ATk Pl* 1×¼ ton truck, 3×M3 halftracks, 3×57mm guns. Three *Rifle Pls* of five squads — three rifle, one mortar and one LMG: each squad 1×M3 halftrack.
Service Coy: *Coy HQ:* HQ Sect 1×¾ ton comd car; AM&S Sect 1×2½ ton truck, 1×1 ton trailer; Maint Sect 1×¼ ton truck, 1×2½ ton truck, 1×1 ton trailer; Bn Admin & Personnel Sect 1×2½ ton truck, 1×1 ton trailer. *Bn Supply & Tptn Pl* 1×¼ ton truck, 1×¾ ton truck, 9×2½ ton trucks, 5×1 ton trailers, 4×M10 ammo trailers. *Bn Maint Pl* 1×¼ ton truck, 1×M3 halftrack, 2×2½ ton trucks, 1×6 ton heavy wrecker, 1×M32 ARV, 2×1 ton trailers.

Fig 22 Armoured Infantry Battalion.

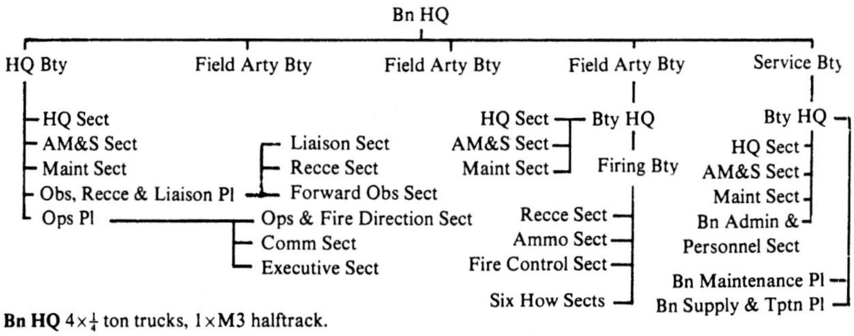

Bn HQ 4×¼ ton trucks, 1×M3 halftrack.
HQ Bty: *Bty HQ:* HQ Sect 1×¼ ton truck; AM&S Sect 1×2½ ton truck, 1×1 ton trailer; Maint Sect 1×¼ ton truck, 1×M3 halftrack, 1×1 ton trailer; Obs, Recce & Liaison Pl: Liaison Sect 1×M3 halftrack; Recce Sect 1×¼ ton truck, 1×M3 halftrack, Forward Obs Sect: 3×M4 tanks. *Ops Pl:* Op & Fire Direction Sect 3×M3 halftracks; Comm Sect 2×¾ ton trucks, 1×M3 halftrack; Exec Sect 1×¼ ton truck, 1×¼ ton trailer, 1×¾ ton truck, 1×M3 halftrack, 2×L5 lt planes.
Field Arty Bty: *Bty HQ:* HQ Sect 1×¼ ton truck, 1×M3 halftrack; AM&S Sect 1×2½ ton truck, 1×1 ton trailer; Maint Sect 1×¼ ton truck, 1×M3 halftrack, 1×1 ton trailer. *Firing Bty:* Recce Sect 1×¼ ton truck, 1×M3 halftrack; Ammo Sect 2×M3 halftracks, 2×M10 ammo trailers; Fire Control Sect 2×M3 halftracks; Six Howitzer Sects each of 1×M7 105mm SP how, 1×M10 ammo trailer.
Service Bty: *Bty HQ:* HQ Sect 1×¾ ton truck; AM&S Sect 1×2½ ton truck, 1×1 ton trailer; Maint Sect 1×¼ ton truck, 1×2½ ton truck, 1×1 ton trailer; Bn Admin & Personnel Sect 1×2½ ton truck, 1×1 ton trailer. *Bn Maint Pl* 1×¼ ton truck, 2×2½ ton trucks, 2×1 ton trailers, 1×6 ton heavy wrecker, 2×M32 ARV. *Bn Supply & Tptn Pl* 1×¼ ton truck, 2×¾ ton trucks, 16×2½ ton trucks, 7×1 ton trailers, 9×M10 ammo trailers.

Fig 23 Armoured Field Artillery Battalion.

Airborne troops inside a C-47 transport aircraft, en route to their dropzone.

Auxiliary units, such as the recce squadron, plus attached medical personnel and unit chaplains, brought the strength to 10,937. As with the infantry division, other battalions such as tank destroyers or AA artillery, were normally attached.

THE AIRBORNE DIVISION

By the start of 1944 the United States had raised, trained and equipped five airborne divisions. The 82nd and 101st were together in England, preparing for D-Day, the 11th was in the Far East and the 13th and 17th still completing training in the USA. To support this powerful airborne force were large numbers of troop carrying C-47 aircraft, deployed in the Army Air Corps Commands in Europe and the Far East. It had taken less than three years to achieve this remarkable expansion, for in June 1941 the *only* airborne unit in existence was the 501st Parachute Battalion. It was mainly thanks to the energy and drive of a small group of enthusiastic pioneers, fully supported in their endeavours by Gen Marshall and Gen Hap Arnold. A key figure in this expansion was Maj-Gen William C. Lee (known as the 'Father of US Airborne Forces'). The success of German parachute troops undoubtedly acted as a spur to US

Organic Components of the Airborne Division of World War II

Div	Inf Regt Glider	Inf Regt Para	Fd Arty Bn Glider	Fd Arty Bn Para	A/B AA Bn	Para Maint Coy	A/B Sig Coy	A/B Ord Coy	A/B QM Coy	A/B Eng Bn	A/B Med Coy
11	187 188	 511	472 675	457 674	152	11	511	711	408	127	221
11	187	188 511	472 675	457 674	152	11	511	711	408	127	221
13	88 326	515	676 677	458	153	13	513	713	409	129	222
13	326	515 517	676 677	458 460	153	13	513	713	409	129	222
17	193 194	513	680 681	466	155	17	517	717	411	139	224
17	194	507 513	630 681	464 466	155	17	517	717	411	139	224
82	325	504 505	319 320	376 456	80	–	82	782	407	307	307
82	325	504 505	319 320	376 456	80	82	82	782	407	307	307
101	327 401	502	321 907	377	81	–	101	801	426	326	326
101	327	502 506	321 907	377 463	81	101	101	801	426	326	326

Note: The first and second lines for each division show the organisation prior to 1 March 1945 and the third and fourth lines show the composition after that date.

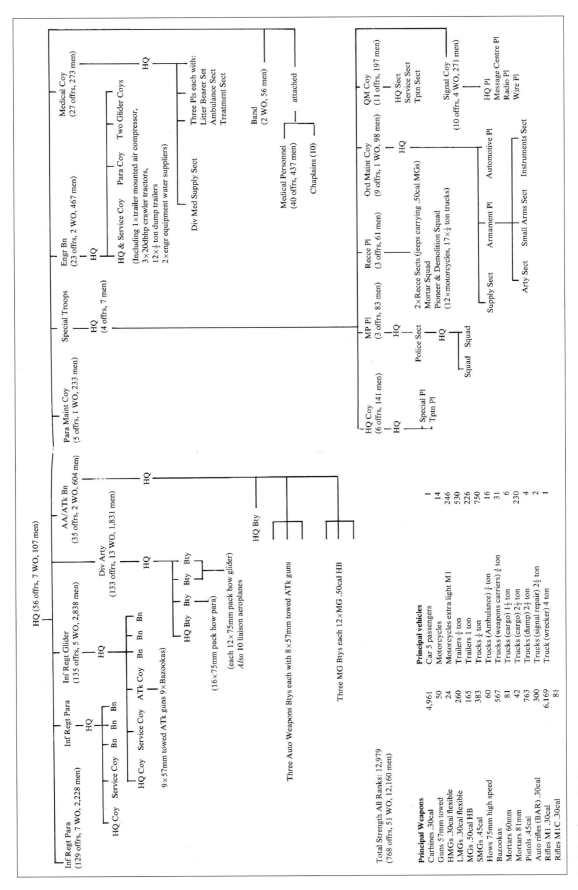

HQ (56 offrs, 7 WO, 107 men)

Inf Regt Para
(129 offrs, 7 WO, 2,228 men)

HQ Coy   Service Coy   HQ   Bn   Bn   Bn

Inf Regt Para

HQ   Bn   Bn   Bn

HQ Coy   Service Coy   ATk Coy   Bn   Bn   Bn

9×57mm towed ATk guns 9×Bazookas)

Inf Regt Glider
(135 offrs, 5 WO, 2,838 men)

HQ

Div Arty
(133 offrs, 13 WO, 1,831 men)

HQ

HQ Bty   Bty   Bty   Bty

HQ Bty   Bty   Bty

(16×75mm pack how para)

(each 12×75mm pack how glider)
Also 10 liaison aeroplanes

AA/ATk Bn
(35 offrs, 2 WO, 604 men)

HQ

HQ Bty

Three Auto Weapons Btys each with 8×57mm towed ATk guns

Three MG Btys each 12×MG .50cal HB

Para Maint Coy
(5 offrs, 1 WO, 233 men)

Special Troops

HQ
(4 offrs, 7 men)

Engr Bn
(23 offrs, 2 WO, 467 men)

HQ

HQ & Service Coy   Para Coy   Two Glider Coys

(Including 1×trailer mounted air compressor,
3×20dbhp crawler tractors,
12×¼ ton dump trailers
2×engr equipment water suppliers)

Div Med Supply Sect

Medical Coy
(27 offrs, 2 WO, 273 men)

HQ

Three Pls each with:
Litter Bearer Set
Ambulance Sect
Treatment Sect

Band
(2 WO, 56 men)

Medical Personnel
(40 offrs, 437 men)

Chaplains (10)

attached

HQ Coy
(6 offrs, 141 men)

HQ

Special Pl
Tptn Pl

MP Pl
(3 offrs, 83 men)

HQ

Police Sect

HQ

Squad   Squad

Squad

Recce Pl
(3 offrs, 61 men)

2×Recce Sects (jeeps carrying .50cal MGs)
Mortar Squad
Pioneer & Demolition Squad
(12×motorcycles, 17×¼ ton trucks)

Ord Maint Coy
(9 offrs, 1 WO, 98 men)

HQ

Supply Sect

Armament Pl

Arty Sect

Automotive Pl

Small Arms Sect

Instruments Sect

QM Coy
(11 offrs, 197 men)

HQ
HQ Sect
Service Sect
Tptn Sect

Signal Coy
(10 offrs, 4 WO, 271 men)

HQ Pl
Message Centre Pl
Radio Pl
Wire Pl

Total Strength All Ranks: 12,979
(768 offrs, 51 WO, 12,160 men)

Principal Weapons	
Carbines .30cal	4,961
Guns 57mm towed	50
HMGs .30cal flexible	24
LMGs .30cal flexible	260
MGs .50cal HB	165
SMGs .45cal	383
Hows 75mm high speed	60
Bazookas	567
Mortars 60mm	81
Mortars 81mm	42
Pistols .45cal	763
Auto rifles (BAR) .30cal	300
Rifles M1 .30cal	6,169
Rifles M1C .30cal	81

Principal vehicles	
Car 5 passengers	1
Motorcycles	14
Motorcycles extra light M1	246
Trailers ¼ ton	530
Trailers 1 ton	226
Trucks ¼ ton	750
Trucks (Ambulance) ¾ ton	16
Trucks (weapons carriers) ¾ ton	31
Trucks (cargo) 1½ ton	6
Trucks (cargo) 2½ ton	230
Trucks (dump) 2½ ton	4
Trucks (signal repair) 2½ ton	2
Truck (wrecker) 4 ton	1

Fig 24 Airborne Division.

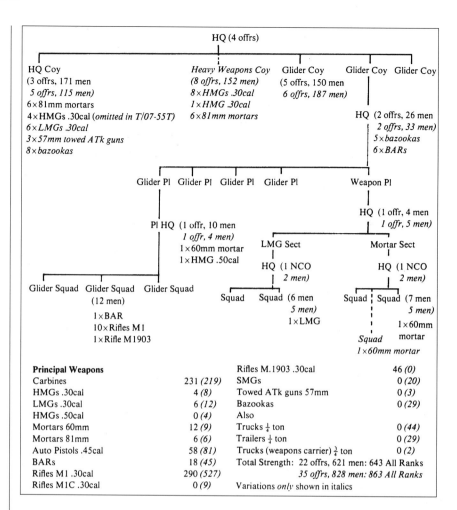

Fig 25 Infantry Battalion Glider. (Source: T/07–55 of September 1942, T/07–55T of 16 September 1944)

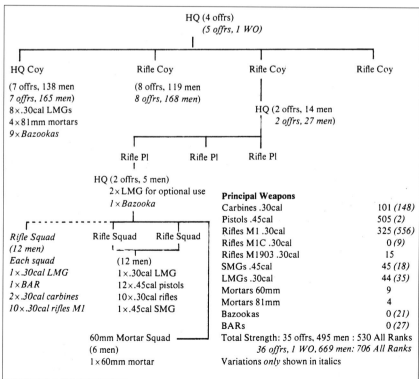

Fig 26 Infantry Battalion Parachute. (Source: T/07–35 of 17 February 1942, T/07–35T of 24 February 1944)

development and expansion. The 82nd (All American) Division, originally a World War I unit, was reactivated in March 1942 and five months later it was split to form the first two airborne divisions – the 82nd and the 101st (Screaming Eagles).

As conceived in 1942, the airborne division was virtually a miniature infantry division, with a total strength of only 8,505 (7,009 fewer than that of the infantry division). However, it contained not only all the usual divisional elements but also a small organic AA battalion. Each division had one parachute infantry regiment (1,985 men compared with 3,333 in an infantry regt) and two glider infantry regiments (each 1,605 men). Weapons were those of the normal infantry division, with a predominance of the lighter types.

Divisional artillery, for example, had 30 X 75mm pack howitzers. Vehicle numbers were drastically reduced, with only 408, towing 239 trailers, compared with 2,000 in a standard infantry division. No organic aircraft were contained in the division, so it depended on the pool of transport planes controlled by the AAF. The organisation of the airborne division remained substantially unchanged for the next two years, although in combat commanders often rearranged their resources to meet a particular situation.

On November 1943, Gen Ridgeway, the CG of 82nd Airborne which had been battle tested in Sicily, proposed considerable increases to bring the size of the division almost up to that of the standard infantry division. He had the support of the ETO, but Gen McNair disagreed, maintaining that if an airborne division was needed (and as we have seen he disliked any 'special' type of division) then it must remain easily transportable. Nothing was done at the time, but the ETO influence, which favoured the use of airborne forces en masse, gradually gained dominance. The new tables (Dec 1944) closely resembled Gen Ridgeway's proposals and represented a 50 per cent increase in manpower to 12,979. Its two parachute and one glider regiments were similar to standard infantry regiments and larger, more developed supporting units were included. The four divisions in Europe (13th, 17th, 82nd and 101st) were all reorganised, but the 11th remained on the old scaling.

Weapons

Every paratrooper carried a .45cal pistol and an M1 rifle, officers mostly carried pistols, but some sensibly preferred rifles or Thompson sub-machine guns. Each man jumped with his personal weapons, but machine guns, mortars, reserve ammunition, radio sets and medical equipment were packed in bundles or 'para-packs' which were either dropped from the six bomb racks under the belly of the Dakota, or pushed out of the door by the jumpmaster.

CAVALRY DIVISIONS

As World War II approached and in particular after the creation of the Armored Force in 1940, 'what to do with the cavalry?' became one of the most perplexing questions. The cavalry division had been in existence for many years and some cavalrymen looked with a mixture of suspicion and dislike upon the impending mechanisation and the demise of the horse as a weapon of war. There were two cavalry divisions active in March 1942 and it was decided to maintain them both as horse units, only mechanising the non divisional cavalry and those elements in armoured and infantry divisions. At that time both cavalry divisions were organised on the old 'square' organisation with a total establishment of some 11,000 men. However, the shipping of horses was so costly in tonnage, and their feeding and upkeep presented such difficulties in a fully motorised army, that no plans were ever made to move the divisions anywhere with their horses. The 2nd Cavalry Division was sent to North Africa early in 1944 only to be inactivated and broken up in May 1944, its personnel being transferred to service units. The 1st Cavalry Division in the SW Pacific was found suitable employment and fought with distinction, but as dismounted infantry.

Although its unique organisation (see table below) raised its strength to almost that of an infantry division, it retained the basic square formation of two cavalry brigades with two regiments in each. It lacked the 155mm field artillery medium howitzer battalion, but was given a special allowance of heavy weapons and other 'infantry type' equipment.

1st Cavalry Division Authorised Strength		Organic Components of the 1st Cavalry Division in World War II	
Entire Div	12,724	Cav Div	1
Div HQ	143	1st Cav Bde Regts	5, 12
Bdes(2)	4,278	2nd Cav Bde Regts	7, 8
(2 cav/inf regts per bde)		Fd Arty Bns	61, 82, 99, 271
Recce Tp	180	Med Sqn	1
Fd Arty	1,920	Sig Tp	1
Auxiliary Units:		Engr Sqn	8
Engr Sqn	636	QM Sqn	16
Med Sqn	397	Ord Coy	27

1st Cavalry Division Authorised Strength		Organic Components of the 1st Cavalry Division in World War II	
QM Tp	186	Recce Tp	302
Ord Coy	176	Tank Coy	603
Sig Tp	239		
MP Pl	106		
Div HQ Tp	127		
Band	58		

MOTORISED DIVISION

The motorised division organisation appeared shortly after Pearl Harbor, with the intention that there should be one for each pair of armoured divisions, the three forming an armoured corps. In its short life the division went through various planning stages, but in general terms it was conceived as an infantry division, equipped with sufficient organic soft skinned transport to lift all its men and materials without shuttling. Also, there would be vehicles for large recce, maintenance and supply elements, so that the division could be tactically independent. From the outset Gen McNair was against the proposal, rightly considering that it was wasteful to assign permanently so much transport organically. In April 1942, four infantry divisions (6th, 7th, 8th and 9th) were supposedly converted to motorised divisions and the 4th and 90th were also converted shortly afterwards. In practice, only the 4th Division was fully equipped with all the appropriate vehicles and equipment. It was earmarked for overseas service in August 1942. However, as it required as much ship tonnage as an armoured division, without having the same firepower, no theatre commander requested it in the months that followed. It is hardly surprising, therefore, that it was viewed with disfavour by the AGF Reduction Board. The question was not about the motorisation of the infantry, but how the trucks to do this should be organised. Infantry could not fight from the trucks which were only used to get them into position for battle. In 1936, when planning the triangular division, the War Department had said that MT for infantrymen should be pooled, and it was to this principle that Gen McNair clung. For a while the Operations Division (OPD) of the War Department was unwilling to do away with the motorised division, believing it was necessary so as to provide proper infantry support for armoured divisions. The raising of the ratio of infantry to tanks within the armoured division obviated this need, and OPD withdrew its objections, subject to the reorganisation of the armoured divisions. All the motorised divisions, except for the 4th Division, were then reconverted to standard infantry. Later, the 4th was also reconverted, after the ETO had confirmed that no motorised division was included in their plans, but that all infantry divisions should receive training in motor movement. The table below shows the outline organisation of the ill fated motorised division.

Motorised Division T/O 77 of 1 August 1942

Entire Div	16,889	Auto Rifles .30cal	642
Div HQ	153	LMGs .30cal	118
Inf Regts (3)	3,427	HMGs .30cal	86
Fd Arty	2,479	MGs .50cal	253
Auxiliary Units:		Mortars 60mm	81
Recce Sqn	838	Mortars 81mm	63
Engr Bn	750	ATk Guns 37mm	108
Med Bn	519	Hows 75mm SP	18
QM Bn	553	How 105mm	6
Ord Coy	146	Hows 155mm	12
Sig Coy	312	Lt Tanks	17
MP Coy	135	Halftracks (w/armament)	10
Div HQ Coy	144	Lt Armd Cars	38
Attached Medical	567	Scouts Cars (w/armament)	3
Attached Chaplain	12	Halftrack APCs (w/armament)	20
		Vehicles All Types	2,879*
		Less Combat Types	2,767
Principal Armament			
Rifles .30cal	5,949		
Rifles M1903 .30cal	810		
Carbines .30cal	6,879		

* This is 730 vehicles more than the existing inf div and 867 more than the planned inf div.

LIGHT DIVISIONS

It was clear in 1942 that the Army must prepare itself for a variety of specialised operations, under extremes of both climate and physical conditions, and also be capable of using specialised means of assault, such as airborne or amphibious operations. The problem was to decide how far to go towards organising special types of division which would perfectly suit just one of these operations, rather than relying upon merely teaching the special skills needed to normal infantrymen. Certainly Gen McNair at HQ AGF favoured the latter approach in the interests of economy and flexibility. Between March and September 1942 the AGF opened four specialised training centres to teach airborne, amphibious, desert and mountain warfare respectively. Each had the job of testing special equipment and supervising the specialised training of such standard units as were allocated to them. No special desert or amphibious forces were ever developed, and for a time no airborne or mountain troops were organised above regimental level. As we have seen already, the airborne division became properly authorised and five airborne divisions formed.

By the summer of 1942 it was also clear that an offensive against the Japanese in the South-West Pacific was now possible, so investigation began into the need for specialised jungle and mountain troops. The standard infantry division was much too heavily equipped to be able to move easily through the roadless terrain of jungles or mountains. After some discussion about where specialised work, such as jungle training, could take place, the War Department, in January 1943, directed AGF to prepare tables for a light division which was capable of operating, if

Heavily-laden men of the 10th Mtn Div, Fifth (US) Army, near Mt Belvedere, Italy, 21 February 1945.

possible, without vehicles and even without animals. Preliminary tables were produced in early March 1943, for a division of about 9,000 men. It had similar components to those of a standard infantry division except they were much smaller. No recce troop was included and the artillery limited to three battalions of 75mm pack howitzers. The divisions were designed for use in mountain, jungle, airborne or amphibious operations, with the attachment of appropriate forms of transport. Organic transportation was limited to handcarts, sledges for cold weather mountain operations, and pack mules or jeeps for the artillery. Other elements would receive additional transportation by the attachment of pack mules, light trucks or native bearers, so that supplies could be fetched from supply points five miles in rear. For airborne operations, light divisions would be trained on gliders and combined with non divisional paratroops. For mountain work they would be reinforced with ski troops, and for amphibious operations they would train on landing craft. Slight variations in personal weapons would allow for more sub-machine guns in the jungle role, more automatic rifles for airborne and amphibious assaults and more M1 rifles for the mountains.

Three light divisions were authorised in June 1943. The 89th Light Division (Truck) was formed by converting the 89th Infantry Division. The 10th Light Division (Pack, Alpine) was activated mainly from the elements trained at the Mountain Training Centre using the 87th Mountain Infantry Regiment as its nucleus. The 71st Light Division

Carrying their weapons and ammunition, GIs wade waist-deep through a stream on Manus, one of the Admiralty islands in the South-West Pacific, March 1944. They are followed by two caterpillar tractors pulling trailers laden with stores.

(Pack, Jungle) was activated from miscellaneous elements, mainly the 5th and 14th Infantry, which had already received jungle training in Panama. Tests of the 71st and 89th culminated in interdivisional manoeuvres in the early spring of 1944. The terrain chosen was a mountainous, virtually roadless, but relatively warm area in California, known as the Hunter Liggett Military Reservation. Reports by 'III' Corps, who umpired and supervised the manoeuvres, were unfavourable. The handcarts proved to be inadequate and fatiguing. Additional pack and truck transport had to be provided to keep the manoeuvres functioning and additional engineers brought in to build tracks for both mules and jeeps. Too many combat soldiers had to be used opening up supply routes and in carrying up supplies, so that neither division could deploy more than six battalions of infantry. In addition, recce forces had to be improvised. The report concluded that the light division was incapable of sustaining itself over any reasonable length of time and recommended the return of the two divisions to normal organisation and equipment. This was accepted and the 71st and 89th reconverted; they were thus among the last divisions to go overseas, not leaving AGF command until January 1945. As it turned out the 71st was used in the ETO (to help stop the German Ardennes offensive) despite its previous jungle training!

Although tests with 10th Light Division (Pack, Alpine) also proved disappointing, the War Department decided to keep the 10th as a special mountain division and the AGF accordingly prepared the necessary tables (see below). These outlined a division of 14,101 all ranks, using over 6,000 horses and mules, but with some MT for long journeys. The 10th Mountain Division embarked for Italy in December 1944. Gen Mark Clark in his book *Calculated Risk*, tells how the division was offered first to the other theatres of war, but turned down because of its specialised equipment. 5th Army, however, was happy to have the division, which included some of the world's best skiers, was equipped with specialised vehicles such as the Weasel, and was ably commanded by Maj-Gen George P. Hays, a Medal of Honor winner from World War I.

Mountain Division T/O 70 of 4 November 1944

Entire Div	14,101	*Principal Armament*	
Div HQ	163	Rifles .30cal	850
Inf Regts (3)	2,872	Carbines .30cal	5,620
Fd Arty	1,738	Auto Rifles .30cal	477
Cav Recce Tp	162	MGs .30cal	204
Engr Bn	782	MGs .50cal	85
Med Bn	665	Mortars 60mm	81
QM Bn	459	Mortars 81mm	54
Ord Coy	91	ATk Rocket Launchers	263
Sig Coy	267	Guns 37mm	27
MP Pl	71	Guns 57mm Towed	18
Div HQ Coy	89	How 75mm Pack	36
ATk Bn	347	Vehicles All Types	680
HQ Special Troops	9	Horses and Mules	6,152
Attached Medical	630		
Attached Chaplain	12		

THE SOLDIER

BADGES AND INSIGNIA

Cap Badges

The coat of arms of the United States of America was worn as a cap badge on the peaked cap by all ranks. However, whereas the officer's version was about 3in X 2.6in (75mm X 65mm), the enlisted men wore a smaller version which was attached to a disc about 1.6in (40mm) in diameter. Both were made of brass or gilded brass. The Women's Army Corps wore a different eagle on its own, while there were special cap badges for warrant officers (an eagle standing on two arrows and a laurel wreath), West Point Academy, Transport Services and military bands (see Fig 27).

Collar Badges

Brass collar badges denoting the arm or service were worn by all ranks, but as with the cap badge, the enlisted man's badge was smaller than the officer's and was attached to a brass disc. Officers wore the collar badges in pairs (except on shirts in summer uniforms when badges of rank took the place of the left hand collar badge), with the US national insignia above the branch badge. Enlisted men wore them singly, with the 'US' on the right and branch badge on the left (see Fig 28).

Army Officers

Harbour Boat Service

WAC

West Point Academy

Warrant Officer

Transport Service

US Army Band

Fig 27 Cap Badges

The photograph shows a good comparison between the officer's uniform and that of the enlisted man. Note, for example, Ike's collar badges, as compared to those of the Staff Sergeant and the fact that his better tailored 'forest green' jacket is much darker. The photograph was taken in the Washington Hotel, a GIs' leave hotel in London in 1942, so Eisenhower was still only a Major-General.

Breast Badges

Fig 29 shows a selection of breast badges. These were awarded for length of service, or exemplary service, in particular arms and worn on either breast (the Combat Infantryman and Army Paratroops badge on the left; the General Staff identification badge on the right).

Rank Badges

Officers
2-Lt One gold bar; 1-Lt One silver bar; Capt Two bars; Maj One gold oak leaf; Lt-Col One Silver oak leaf; Col An eagle with an arrow in its claws; Brig One star; Maj-Gen Two stars; Lt-Gen Three stars; Gen Four stars; General of the Army Five stars in a circle surmounted by an eagle. The full colonel's silver eagle gave rise to the expression 'Bird Colonels'.

Surprisingly, silver always ranked above gold, and all badges (unless indicated otherwise) were in silver.

NCOs
During World War II a new set of enlisted grades, known as 'technicians', was introduced, and designated by incorporating the letter T with the chevrons as worn by normal line NCOs. As Fig 30 shows, there was one exception, namely the top grade technical sergeant. Master sergeant and

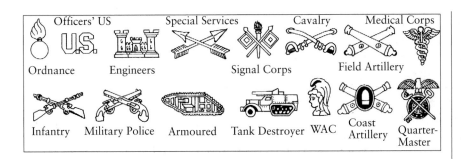

Fig 28 A Selection of Officers' Collar Badges

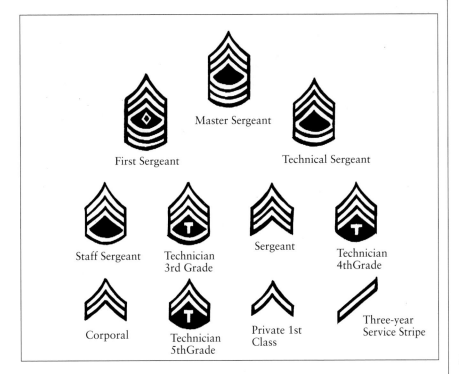

Fig 29 A Selection of Breast Badges

Fig 30 NCOs' Rank Badges

first sergeant were merely dependent upon the appointment held and had equal rank. All rank badges were 3.2in (80mm) wide in light khaki or light yellow silk on dark blue material.

Shoulder Insignia

An enormous number of different shoulder patches were worn during World War II. Appendix 8 at the end of the book gives details of all divisional shoulder insignia, battle honours and nicknames.

Although these four officers are USAAF (pictured here before a court martial in the UK (two on left are defending counsel, two on right trial judge and asst)), they all wear the standard Class 'A' US Army officer's pattern service dress, with dark forest green jacket and lighter trousers (known as 'pinks' from the tinge of red in their beige colour), plus peaked cap (complete with officer's capbadge) and brown shoes. Only the trial judge wears his leather belt with cross-strap (cf: British 'Sam Browne') and two service stripes at the bottom of his left sleeve.

Badges and Insignia in Combat

As a general rule, badges of rank or insignia denoting type of unit, etc. were kept to a minimum on combat dress. Sometimes officers and NCOs wore their rank painted on the front of steel helmets, but this was a dead giveaway for enemy snipers; in other cases it was painted on the rear. Other signs found on helmets included divisional flashes, red crosses in white discs for medical personnel and broad white bands with the letters MP in the front of Military Police helmets. On combat dress the only unit insignia to be worn universally were divisional shoulder patches.

DRESS

In 1941 the US Army was, after years of peacetime garrison soldiering, ill prepared to clothe and equip its GIs for battle all over the world under all types of climatic conditions. Incidentally, the term 'GI' was coined from the initials of the 'Government Issue' stamp normally found on all issue (cf. 'WD' and the broad arrow used by the British War Department). Uniforms had not changed much since those worn by the doughboys of the AEF in World War I, the most easily recognisable items being the headgear – the British type steel helmet and the 'Boy Scout' style soft hat. By 1944, however, the US soldier was undoubtedly the best and most sensibly dressed of all the combatants, thanks to the care put into designing his clothing and equipment. Despite some shortages, the American GI had much to be thankful for. For example, the USA was the first nation to issue its soldiers with separate clothing to fight in, to that issued for parade and walking out. While the British had to make the best of battledress for virtually every activity in temperate climes, the American combat jacket was the first real attempt by any nation to design a special item of clothing for battle. Even the Germans had to fight in a tailored, badged and braided tunic for most of the war. Another milestone was the principle adopted of providing layers of clothing so that the same basic combat uniform could be worn winter and summer, with or without woollen liners, sweaters, hoods, etc. which were worn when necessary.

TEMPERATE DRESS

The GIs non combat service dress consisted of an open-necked tunic with four straight flapped pockets, a pair of straight trousers, brown leather boots or shoes, plus a peaked cap or the envelope type 'overseas' cap. All clothing was olive drab in colour but varied considerably in tone. Shirts and ties ranged from olive to light tan. Officers wore a similar service dress, but with a dark worsted wool band around each cuff, which was the mark of an officer of any rank. Later in the war the 'Ike' jacket was also worn by officers. This resembled the British battledress blouse, but had many variations in colour, cut and style. This then was the uniform the GI wore on and off duty and it is no wonder that the British Tommies were envious.

For battle the GIs wore on their heads the M1 steel helmet, apart from tank crews who had a special tank crew crash helmet, and airborne troops who wore a slightly modified version of the regular steel helmet. The helmet was in three parts: the outer steel shell, usually painted olive drab, sometimes worn with a scrim net for taking camouflage material and fitted with an adjustable chinstrap. This fitted snugly over the top of a composite liner of a similar shape, but slightly smaller size, with an inner cradle of straps to grip the head. The third element was an olive knit cap, known as a 'beanie', designed to be worn under the helmet, but often worn on its own as it made a comfortable, warm, but casual, form of headgear. The GI often outdid the British soldier in his casual way of dressing – that was until a commander of the calibre of Gen George S. Patton Jr arrived on the scene to smarten them up! The outer helmet was an ideal washing bowl, cooking pot, an emergency entrenching tool, in fact its uses were legion, depending only on the inventiveness of the wearer!

Shirts were olive drab with attached collars and two patch pockets; they were usually worn open at the neck. Over the shirt was worn the M1941 Field Jacket which was hip length, or the thigh length M1943 Field Jacket. The latter was infinitely superior, being windproof, waterproof and tear resistant (the former was windproof only). With concealed zip fasteners,

Bailing rainwater out of an AA machine gun emplacement is a novel use for the M1 steel helmet! This photograph shows all three elements that made up the GIs' battle headgear, namely: the steel outer, the composite liner which could be worn on its own and the olive-knit 'beanie', which Gen George Patton hated!

good large pockets and other attractive features, the jackets were excellent, a button-in liner and hood being added for winter. The M1943 Field Dress also had trousers and a simple peaked cloth cap in the same material, but the olive drab service dress trousers had to be worn with the M1941 jacket. Calf legging gaiters were initially worn with the brown leather boots, but these were replaced by a new boot which appeared in 1944. This had a built-in leather gaiter, which was fastened with two small straps and buckles. In 1945 yet another high boot appeared, which, like the paratrooper's boot on which it was modelled, laced all the way up to the lower calf.

Other miscellaneous clothing included long greatcoats and raincoats, high necked pullovers, scarves and balaclava helmets, herringbone twill suits (for mechanics and armoured unit personnel), rubber storm boots with snap metal clips, and olive wool or brown leather gloves. In addition to their crash helmets, tank crewmen wore the highly sought after short windcheater jackets, over the top of their baggy, one-piece overalls. Improvised white snow camouflage hooded jackets and overtrousers were used but were not in general issue. The two piece tropical camouflage uniform was worn for a time in the ETO in the summer of 1944, but was unfortunately very similar to the German Waffen-SS dress, which led to a number of fatal errors.

These Rangers, using a Red Cross coffee stall on the seafront at Weymouth, Dorset, while loading for D-Day, wear the standard temperate climate combat dress and are festooned with weapons and equipment, including deflated M-1926 US Navy lifebelts around their waists. (National Archives)

Snow-suits had to be worn for camouflage on the Western Front in the winter of 1944/5, but most were locally produced. These 7th (US) Army GIs are on patrol in the Domaniale forest south of Bitche on the Strasbourg front, 15 January 1945.

TROPICAL DRESS

The GIs and Marines of the peacetime Pacific garrisons wore the normal hot weather service uniforms, consisting of a shirt and trousers in light tan or khaki drill material which was known as 'chino'. It was patently unsuitable for battle, but a satisfactory jungle uniform did not go into full production until nearly the end of the war; consequently interim solutions had to be found. The first was to use the olive green twill fatigues, which had been introduced to replace the old blue working denims. The first real jungle suit was delivered in late 1942 and consisted of a baggy, one piece garment, camouflaged on one side in jungle colours, and either plain tan or camouflaged in sandy browns, on the other. The latter was intended for beach or open country wear. This single piece garment was very unpopular, as GIs virtually had to undress to wash or answer a call of nature, so a two piece suit was introduced. However, the camouflage pattern made the wearer easier to see when he was moving and it was eventually replaced in 1944, by a herringbone twill two piece olive drab green jungle suit, which became the most commonly worn combat dress for the rest of the war. A new lightweight two piece jungle suit, made of olive green poplin, was introduced in the spring of 1945. Camouflaged helmet covers were worn with all these later forms of dress, particularly by Marine units.

SPECIALISED CLOTHING

Armoured Units

In addition to normal army clothing, tankers were issued with four special items: a World War I pilot's type of fabric tight fitting helmet with housings for earphones – universally disliked by all! Secondly a composition crash helmet with a padded and ventilated top and earpieces, which was generally liked and worn in preference to the steel helmet.

GIs wearing lightweight jungle suits disembark at a New Guinea port. Note the extra ammunition bandoliers and musette bags.

This group of 4th Armd Div tankers, taken at Devizes, Wilts., in May 1944, all wear the coveted zippered windcheater, composition crash helmet and earphones. Note also their webbing belts and straps, but none of them carries his personal weapons. (Col James Leach)

One piece olive drab herringbone twill overalls were universally worn from 1942 onwards, there being two slightly different versions. The last item was the zipped windcheater, which, as I have already explained, was a much sought after item by every seasoned campaigner, no matter what his branch of the army. It was comfortable, warm and weatherproof. With a zip from top to bottom, knitted cuffs and waistband, it lacked only shoulder straps – so officers had to pin their rank badges directly on to the jacket.

Airborne Units

Steel helmets, designated the M1C, were suitably modified so that they would act as a crash helmet as well as providing battlefield protection. This included the addition of extra harness inside and a moulded chin-cup. A special airborne combat jacket and trousers were worn, both in light brown. The jacket had four distinctive large patch pockets with flaps. It was fastened by a full length covered, heavy duty metal zip. The collar was fastened at the neck by press studs as were the cuffs. Airborne combat trousers were similar to normal combat ones, but had extra large and very distinctive pockets on the thighs, which made them baggy. This is reputed to be why the Germans called the US airborne troops 'Butchers in Baggy Pants'. Airborne jump boots finished off the basic outfit and were one of the most distinctive marks of the airborne soldier, so they were far from pleased when the rest of the Army were issued with very similar high-laced boots. Gen Sir Napier Crookenden gives this graphic description of a fully laden paratrooper in his book *Dropzone Normandy*:

The men of the two US airborne divisions were well equipped for their task, except that the age old tendency persisted to overload the individual soldier in attempt to allow for every emergency. Impregnated combination vest and long drawers were issued to each man, but they were so stiff and scratchy to wear that most men threw them away as soon as they had a chance to take their clothes off. The combat jacket and trousers were sensible, shower-proof and comfortable, and in the baggy pockets of the jacket and trousers a pocket knife, spoon, razor, socks, cleaning patches, torch, maps, rations and ammunition were carried. Each man had a three days of "K" rations, . . . an emergency "D" ration of chocolate, a compass, two fragmentation grenades, one Hawkins anti-tank mine, one smoke grenade and a Gammon bomb* . . . The American soldier topped his uniform with a webbing belt and braces, carrying a .45cal pistol, water canteen, shovel, first aid kit and bayonet. Over all this went his parachute harness, his main parachute in its back-pack and his reserve parachute hooked up in front. A gas mask was strapped to his left leg and a jump knife to his right leg. Under his reserve parachute was slung his musette bag with his spare clothing and ammunition and over the top of everything his Mae West life jacket. Finally, he put on his helmet liner and helmet and picked up his M1 rifle – if he could.

*A home-made anti-tank weapon invented by Lt Jock Gammon of British 1st Parachute Brigade, consisting basically of 2lb of plastic explosive in a black stockinette bag, and a cylinder of gun cotton the size of a cotton reel with an igniter down the centre.

Helped by two of his buddies, a paratrooper buckles into his kit. The dark box-like shape on his chest is the muzzle-end of his Thompson sub-machine gun, to the side of which an extra magazine has been taped. The paratrooper on the left has his carbine (M1A1 with folding stock) in a webbing holster, while the other has a pistol in a shoulder-holster.

PERSONAL EQUIPMENT

As the diagrams of Fig 31 show, the basic webbing worn by all enlisted men – and by the majority of officers in combat – consisted firstly of a broad webbing belt which was fastened in front in a very similar manner to its British equivalent, by a blackened metal fastener. The cartridge or magazine belt had five thin webbing pouches on each side of the buckle (each held a clip of rifle ammunition), a first aid pouch and a canteen, but of course the wearer could choose to add or substitute other items. For those who did not normally carry rifles – tank crews, machine gunners and officers – there was a pistol belt for the big Colt .45 cal and two spare magazines. Both belts had plenty of metal eyelets top and bottom so that extra items could be attached. These included webbing shoulder braces which crossed diagonally in the centre of the back, came vertically down over the shoulders to the top of the chest and then divided into two narrower sections. These were either both fastened to eyelets in the top edge of the belt, or one set could be carried back under the arm and attached to the pack harness. An earlier form of haversack with these straps built in is also shown in the diagrams. Most riflemen carried a bayonet – the one for the Springfield rifle being considerably longer – it was used far more frequently as a combat tool, for example for digging, probing for mines, etc. than for killing the enemy, although it could be used for this purpose most effectively.

Additional items carried included ammunition bandoliers and the ubiquitous all purpose canvas haversack known as a 'musette', which could be slung around the body and worn in the most comfortable position. Early in the war a gas mask satchel was always carried, but tended to be discarded after D-Day. Items such as bayonets, entrenching tools, binoculars, map cases, etc. all had regulation places to be carried, but as the photos show, individuals appear to have pleased themselves. Many GIs added items of enemy equipment to their personal equipment.

Just to show that the US Army was not entirely devoid of 'bull', I have included a kit plate layout from an early edition of the 'Soldier's Manual', it should at least gladden the heart of any sergeant-major!

PERSONAL WEAPONS

In this section I will cover those small arms carried by individual soldiers, namely pistols, rifles, carbines and sub-machine guns. All other small arms, grenades, etc. are covered with the other infantry weapons in Chapter Nine.

Automatic pistol, .45 cal M19111 and M1911A

The pistol is a recoil operated, magazine fed, self loading hand weapon. The magazine holds seven rounds and the pistol weighs about 2.5lb (1.1kg). It was carried in a russet leather holster which was usually accompanied by a webbing pouch holding two spare magazines. The pistol was very powerful, but difficult to fire with any accuracy. Other pistols issued to US forces included a .45cal Smith & Wesson revolver, a .45cal Colt revolver

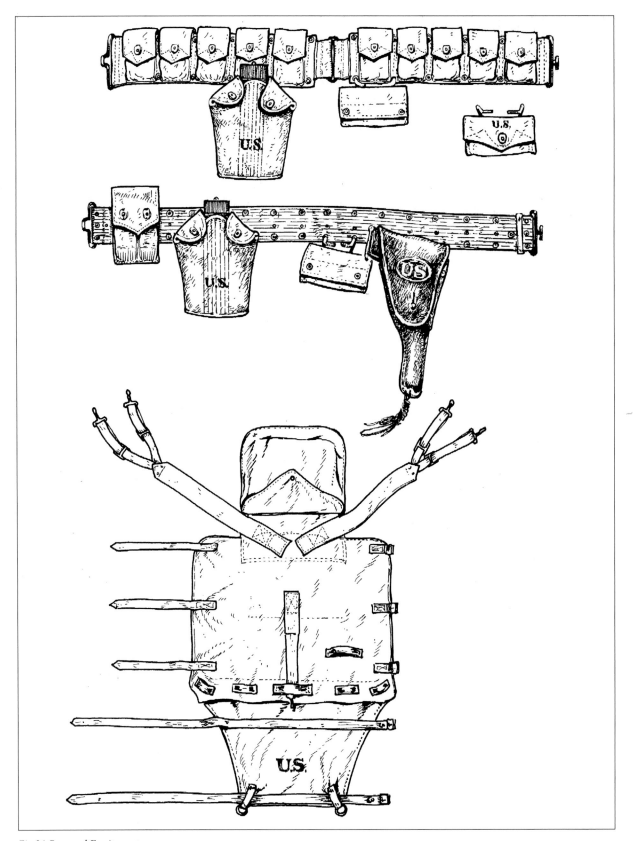

Fig 31 Personal Equipment

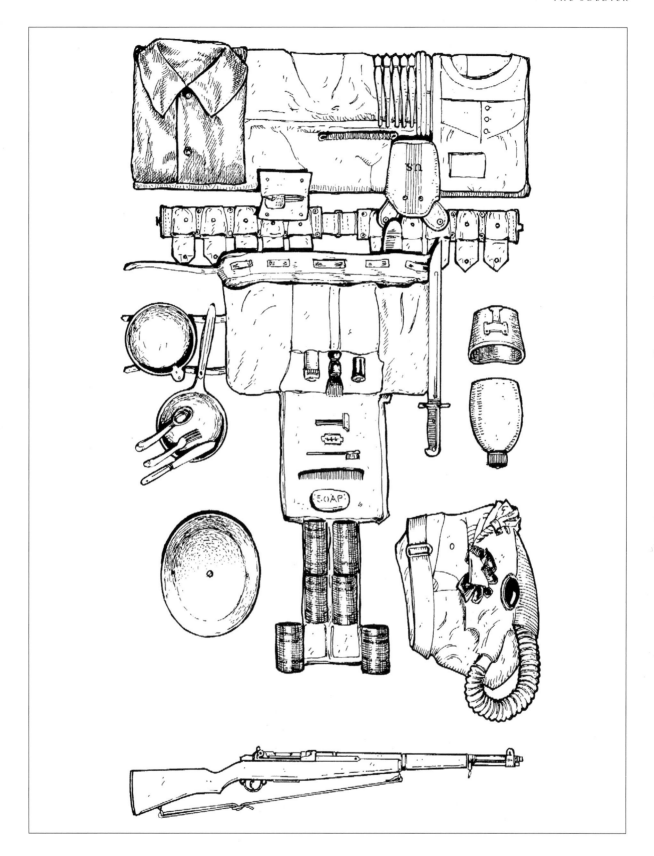

Good close-up of the bayonet on the .30 M1 Garand rifle, together with the rifleman's type belt (each ammo pouch holds a clip of 8 rounds). This GI is Medal of Honor winner, Cpl Charles E. 'Commando' Kelly of 36th Inf Div.

Good close-up of the US Magazine Rifle, cal .30 Model 1903. Known as the Springfield, it was still in widespread use despite the arrival of the Garand and the carbine, many soldiers appreciating its greater accuracy at longer ranges. It was also used as a sniper's rifle when fitted with a telescopic sight. This GI carries the A1 version (with the pistol grip stock).

(both these were M1917 models) and an odd little single shot pistol called the M1942 Liberator.

Magazine Rifle, .30cal, M1903 and M1903A1

Used in World War I, this rifle was still preferred by many soldiers to the Garand. It weighed 9lb (4.1kg), could be fitted with a long 1905 pattern bayonet, and had a magazine capacity of five rounds. There was a sniper's version of the rifle fitted with the Weaver telescopic sight.

Rifle, .30cal, M1

The US infantryman's basic weapon of World War II was the .30cal (7.62mm) M1 semi-automatic, gas operated rifle, which entered mass production in 1939. It had an effective range of about 500yd (max range was over 3,000yd) and a cyclic rate of fire of 20 rounds per minute. A trained soldier could thus fire the eight rounds in his magazine in about 20sec. By 1945 over 5½ million Garands (called after its designer) had been made.

Carbine, .30cal, M1 and M1A1

For those not armed with rifles, the Winchester self-loading carbine was introduced. Much lighter (5.2lb instead of 9.5lb), it had a magazine capacity of either 15 or 30 rounds. Probably the most popular weapon of

A jeep crew 'fire' their self-loading Garand rifles and .30cal Browning machine gun at incoming enemy aircraft, during manoeuvres in Australia. They are wearing leather boots with high leather gaiter tops attached rather than the more normal brown leather boots and webbing pattern gaiters. They also appear to be wearing riding breeches.

World War II – over 6 million carbines of all types were produced. It had a high rate of fire (30rpm) but was not as accurate as the rifle. A later M2 version had a fully automatic capability.

Sub-machine gun, .45cal M1 and M1A1

The .45cal (11.43mm) Thompson M1 weighed about 10.5lb (4.74kg), slightly lighter than the earlier 1928 model beloved of the Chicago gangsters, which was usually fitted with a 50-round drum magazine. It was an expensive weapon with a high rate of fire (600–700rpm) and was followed by a simpler modified version in 1942, the new version taking only the 20- or 30-round box magazine and having no front pistol grip. Despite its weight and size it remained a very popular weapon throughout the war.

Sub-machine gun, .45cal, M3

Lighter than the M1 (8.5lb), the M3 resembled the British Sten, but had certain significant differences. For example the feed was vertical (from a 30-round magazine). It was a reliable, efficient but ugly weapon, with a maximum range of about 100yd and a cyclic rate of fire of 350–540rpm. Fire was automatic only, although an experienced operator could squeeze off single shots. It was, of course, much cheaper to produce and could if necessary be adapted to take 9mm Parabellum ammunition.

Inspecting his carbine in snowy conditions, this GI of Third (US) Army clearly understands how important it is to keep his weapon clean and serviceable. Not as accurate as a rifle, the carbine had a higher rate of fire (30 rounds per minute).

A Ranger cuddles his Thompson sub-machine gun, which is the new M1A1 version without front pistol grip and taking the 20/30-round box magazine instead of the 50-round drum.

Firing the lighter M3 sub-machine gun, which was much cheaper to produce than the Thompson, but was not nearly as popular.

Rations

There were five basic types of field rations in the US Army, known by the letters A, B, C, D and K:

Field Ration A
Almost the same as the garrison ration and the diet of soldiers in the USA. It contained about 70 per cent fresh foods.

Field Ration B
Similar to A, except that nonperishable items were substituted for fresh, such as canned meats, fruits and vegetables, dehydrated potatoes and eggs. As more refrigerated space became available on cargo ships, more fresh foods were shipped overseas. B ration was sometimes called 'Ten in one' as it consisted of enough food for ten men for one day. Two hot and one cold meals could be served from this pack.

Field Ration C
Developed just before the war and replaced the reserve ration of World War I. It consisted of small cans of meat and vegetables (ten in all – meat and beans, meat and vegetable stew, meat and spaghetti, ham, eggs and potatoes, meat and noodles, meat and rice, frankfurters and beans, pork and beans, ham and lima beans, chicken and vegetables). Jam, crackers, powdered drinks, sugar, cereals, etc. were also included.

Two-man 'pup' tents (made by putting together two shelter halves – one carried by each man), provided adequate accommodation, but clearly the slit trench with substantial overhead cover, seen to the rear, was essential in the battle area.

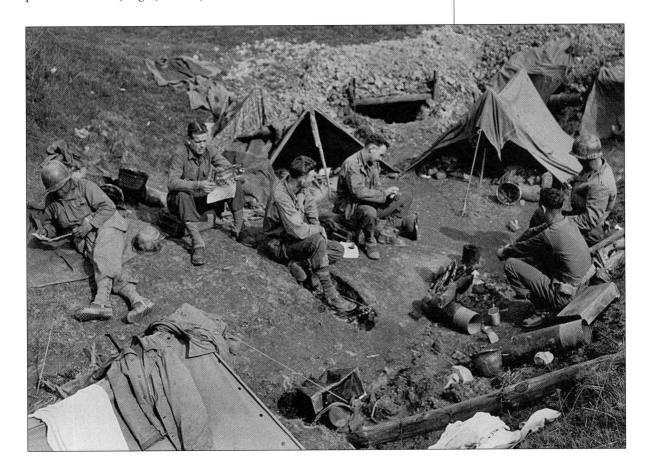

A tired-looking tank crew enjoy a brew-up at the side of their Sherman, after five days of almost non-stop fighting in the Anzio beach-head, Italy.

Soldiers of the 7th Inf Div, operating on Attu in the Aleutian Islands, line up for a hot meal before heading up to the front. (via Real War Photos)

Field Ration D

A highly concentrated chocolate bar, containing cocoa, oat flour and skim milk powder, weighing four ounces. Containing 600 calories, it was for emergency use only, replacing the World War I emergency iron ration.

Field Ration K

Originally developed during the war for paratroops, but was soon very familiar to all front line troops. One meal was packed in a cardboard box 6½in long and waterproofed. The boxes were marked either breakfast, dinner or supper. Breakfast contained a fruit bar, Nescafé, sugar, crackers and a small tin of ham and eggs. Dinner and supper contained a can of cheese or potted meat, crackers, orange or lemon powder, sugar, chocolate or other sweets and chewing gum.

Both C and K rations could be eaten cold or heated if preferred and battle conditions permitted. Each man usually carried one or two meals on his person, while all vehicles had more K rations on board. Many GIs carried paraffin pocket heaters or candles, and small gasoline stoves were issued to outposts, wire crews and other small groups. All units had large two gasoline ranges and, whenever possible, kitchens were set up as explained in Chapter Six. Frequently in the preparation of hot meals a mixture of the various rations would be used.

DECORATIONS AND SERVICE MEDALS

Excluding the Purple Heart, which a wounded soldier often received right at the forward dressing station, the Army awarded 1,400,409 decorations for gallantry and meritorious service. The nation's highest award, the Congressional Medal of Honor, was made to 239 men, more than 40 per cent of whom died in their heroic service. In all, 3,178 Distinguished Service Crosses, 630 Distinguished Service Medals, 7,192 awards of the Legion of Merit, 52,831 Silver Stars, 103,762 Distinguished Flying Crosses, 8,592 Soldier's Medals, 189,309 Bronze Stars and 1,034,676 Air Medals were awarded. Exclusive of the Air Medal and the Purple Heart, the Infantry received 34.5 per cent of all decorations, the Air Corps 34.1 per cent, the Field Artillery 10.7 per cent, Medical personnel 6.0 per cent and all other arms and services 14.7 per cent. For a selection of medals see Fig 32.

UNIT AWARDS

Unit awards were authorised as recognition of certain types of service, usually during a war and as a means of promoting *esprit de corps*. They were of the following categories – unit decorations, infantry streamers, campaign streamers, war service streamers and campaign silver bands. Unit decorations in descending order of precedence were: Distinguished Unit Citation, Presidential Unit Citation (Navy), Meritorious Unit Commendation and Navy Unit Commendation.

Gen Mark Clark stands proudly beside three of his Fifth Army heroes. The centre one has just received the Congressional Medal of Honor; the other two, Distinguished Service Crosses.

Gen George S. Patton Jr wearing all his medals and decorations, which included the DSC with Oak Leaf Cluster, DSM with two Oak Leaf Clusters, Silver Star with Oak Leaf Cluster, Legion of Merit, Bronze Star, plus numerous foreign decorations such as the KBE and CB from Great Britain.

Purple Heart Ribbon: Purple edged in white. Medal: Bronze bust on a purple background surrounded by bronze border, surmounted by a shield with red stars and bars on a white background with, on either side, green leaves.
/R. Wilcockson

Legion of Merit Ribbon: Dusky pink edged in white. Medal: Gold stars on a dark blue background in the centre; main body of medal white with dark red borders; background gold with grass green border.
/R. Wilcockson

Distinguished Service Cross: Ribbon: Royal blue bordered in dark red, these two colours divided by two white stripes. Medal: Dull gold (bronze).
/R. Wilcockson

Fig 32 Medals.

SERVICE MEDALS

These were awarded to members of the Armed Forces to denote the honourable performance of duty in a particular theatre of war for a specified duration. The following service medals were authorised for the period of World War II, including the national emergency period preceding the actual declaration of war:

American Defense Service Medal must have 12 months or more service between 8 September 1939 and 7 December 1941, the period of national emergency.

Women's Army Corps Service Medal must have service in either the WAAC or the WAC.

American Campaign Medal must have at least one year's aggregate service or specified service within the American theatre.

Asiatic Campaign Medal must have active service, 30 days continuous or 60 days not consecutive service in the theatre.

European – African – Middle Eastern Campaign must have similar service as above but within the theatre limits as shown.

World War Two Victory Medal Honourable service between 7 December 1941 and 31 December 1946 (no length specified).

Army of Occupation Medal 30 days consecutive service while assigned to armies of occupation in Germany or Austria, Italy or Japan (specific dates were laid down).

Title of Decoration	For Valor or Achievement	Awarded For
Medal of Honor	Valor	Gallantry and intrepidity at the risk of life above and beyond the call of duty
Distinguished Service Cross	Valor	Extraordinary heroism in military operations against an armed enemy
Distinguished Service Medal	Achievement	Exceptionally meritorious service in a duty of great responsibility
Silver Star	Valor	Gallantry in action
Legion of Merit	Achievement	Exceptionally meritorious conduct in the performance of outstanding service
Distinguished Flying Cross	Valor	Heroism or extraordinary achievement while participating in aerial flight
Soldier's Medal	Valor	Heroism not involving actual conflict with the enemy
Bronze Star Medal	Valor & Achievement	Heroic or meritorious achievement or service against the enemy not including aerial flight
Air Medal	Achievement	Meritorious achievement while participating in aerial flight
Commendation Ribbon	Achievement	Meritorious achievement not in military operations
Purple Heart	Valor	Wounds received in action against an enemy of the United States

WEAPONS, VEHICLES AND EQUIPMENT

INFANTRY WEAPONS

Individual small arms having been dealt with in the last chapter, the remaining infantry type weapons are covered here. They were, of course, used by other arms as well as the infantry.

MACHINE GUNS

Browning Automatic Rifle (BAR) .30in (7.62mm). First developed in 1917, the Model 1919A2 BAR was used in World War II as the infantry squad support weapon.

Length: 47.8in (121.4cm)
Weight: 19.4lb (8.73kg)
Rate of Fire: 500–600rpm or 300–350rpm
Type of Feed: 20rd box magazine

US Machine Gun .30in M1917A1. Standard support weapon for the US Army in World War II. Water-cooled, it resembled the British Vickers in many respects.

Length: 38.64in (98cm)
Weight: 85.75lb (38.5kg) complete less water
Rate of Fire: 450–600rpm
Type of Feed: 250rd fabric or metal link belt

US Machine Gun .30in M1919. The major difference between this gun and the M1917 model was the air-cooled barrel. It was one of the most widely used machine guns in World War II, in AFVs as well as by the infantry. The M1919A4 was the infantry weapon, the A5 for AFVs and

Good view of a Browning Automatic Rifle, belonging to a machine gunner, atop an M3 half-track near the Remagen Bridge, 9 March 1945. He readies his .50 HMG for possible AA use. (via Real War Photos)

Men of the 1st Cav Div firing a water-cooled M1917A1 Browning Machine Gun on the Castner Range, Fort Bliss, Texas, June 1941. (via Real War Photos)

Firing from the hip! Ike tries out a .30in M1919 Browning Machine Gun, but it was more usual to fire it from a bipod in the ground role.

the A6 was used as an infantry squad weapon, having a bipod, butt and carrying handle.

Length: 41in (104cm)
Weight: 31lb (13.95kg)
Rate of Fire: 450–500rpm
Type of Feed: 250rd fabric or metal link belt

Browning .50in (12.7mm) M2. First produced in 1921, this was basically an enlarged version of the .30cal M1917; it had many uses both in the air and on the ground (AFVs, AA and infantry) and was produced in greater quantity than any other US MG in World War II.

Length: 65.1in (165.4cm)
Weight: 84lb (37.8kg)
Rate of Fire: 450–575rpm
Type of Feed: 110rd metal link belt

MORTARS

60mm Mortar M2. The standard light infantry mortar of the American forces. It fired mainly HE rounds but could also fire the M83 illuminating round.

Men of the 1st Inf Div on training early in World War II, set up their 81mm M1 mortar in the New River training area, North Carolina. (via Real War Photos)

WEAPONS, VEHICLES AND EQUIPMENT

Barrel Length: 28.6in (72.6cm)
Range: 100–1,985yd (91–1,816m)
Weight in Action: 42lb (19.07kg)
Bomb Weight: 3lb (1.36kg)

81mm Mortar M1. This mortar fired a variety of projectiles by using up to six charge increments. Not only was it hand carried into action (by two men), but also by special mule packs or in the M6A1 hand cart. It was also mounted on the halftrack mortar carrier M4 and other vehicles.

Barrel Length: 49.5in (125.7cm)
Range: 100–3,290yd (91–3,010m)
Weight in Action: 136lb (61.7kg)
Bomb Weight: HE 6.87lb (3.12kg) and 10.62lb (4.82kg)
      Chemical 10.75lb (4.88kg)

Other types of mortar used by the US Army were: the 4.2in which was the standard weapon of the Chemical Warfare Service (CWS) for firing chemical rounds (smoke and gas). However it was primarily employed as an infantry support weapon, firing a variety of HE and chemical bombs (see Chapter Six for further information on the CWS). Two other mortars were introduced in 1944 – the 105mm T12 and 155mm T25. Very few of

The standard 60mm M2 light infantry mortar in action in Italy, manned by men of one of the famous Nisei (Japanese Americans) Battalions of the 34th Inf Div in Italy.

A 4.2in mortar in action. Men of Co 'B' 91st Chemical Bn operate a 4.2in mortar, to produce a smokescreen to cover the troops of the 5th Inf Div crossing the Sauer River, 8 February 1945. (via Real War Photos)

Loading a bazooka during training. One of the most original weapons ever made, it had a dangerous back blast, but was most effective against AFVs.

the former were ever made and it was never used in action. A few of the latter were used in the SW Pacific, but they were difficult to handle and were withdrawn.

Good comparison shot of the M1 and M9 bazookas, showing how the latter breaks into two pieces for ease of carrying.

ROCKETS

Rocket Launcher M1 and M9 Bazooka. The American Bazooka was one of the most original weapons ever produced (the Germans copied it in their Raketenpanzerbüchse 43 series). It needed a two man team (one firing, one loading) and had a dangerous back blast area which had to be avoided. Nearly half a million bazookas were produced in World War II. The M9 could be broken into two halves for carrying.

Length: 5ft 1in (155cm)
Max Range: 700yd (640m)
Weight of Rocket: 3.4lb (1.53kg)
Penetration of Armour: 4.7in (11.75cm) at 90°

See also Tank section for Calliope (tank mounted rockets) and Artillery section for truck-mounted T27 Multiple Rocket Launchers.

CHEMICAL WEAPONS

Apart from the CWS, the regular troops had to deal with three main types of chemical weapons – gas, smoke and flamethrowers. Illustrated below is a smoke-generating machine. There were three basic types of portable flamethrower used; the M1, M1A1 and M2-2. All were similar in appearance with two fuel tanks and a pressure tank.

Data: M1
Weight: About 70lb (31.8kg)
Range: 25–30yd (22.9–27.4m)
Fuel: 4gal (18.2 litres)
Duration of Fire: 8–10sec

GRENADES

There were two main types of US hand grenade: the M2A1 fragmentation grenade which was shaped like a pineapple and had its outer surface divided into segments like the British Mills 36 grenade. It weighed 1.31lb (0.6kg) and had a 4sec fuse. The second type was the M3A fragmentation grenade which was cylindrical, weighed 0.84lb (0.28kg) and had a 4–5sec fuse.

Refilling a smoke-generating machine. This produced a veil of steam mixed with oil spray, which provided a most effective 'smokescreen'.

M2–2 Flamethrowers being used in action. All three portable flamethrowers (M1, M1A1 and M2–2) comprised two fuel tanks and a pressure tank (carried on the back). The M2–2 had a range of 25–40yd.

M3 Halftracks belonging to the 1st Inf Div on manoeuvres in Devon, 4 May 1944. A fitters' recovery vehicle appears to be towing the rearmost halftrack out of a ditch. (via 1st Inf Div Museum)

ARMOURED VEHICLES

Halftracks

The halftrack personnel carrier T14 which was produced in the late 1930s was the prototype for all the wide variety of halftracks produced by the USA during the war years; it soon became standardised as the M2. There were many variations, only one of which is detailed below, but other basic models included carriers of the 81mm and 4.2in mortars, 75mm and 105mm howitzers, the 57mm gun and various AA mounts including the 40mm Bofors and multiples – twin .50cal MGs, four .50cal MGs and a 37mm cannon plus twin .50cal MGs. The halftrack was originally conceived as a recce vehicle, with adequate protection against small arms and a good cross-country performance. It was widely used throughout the army for a variety of jobs. The basic M2 model was intended as an artillery gun tower for the 105mm howitzer. The M3 model was produced concurrently with the M2 and was the basic personnel carrier. It was armed with a .50cal MG on a pedestal mount and had seats for 10 men, so it could carry a rifle squad in the rear, and had a crew of three.

The Armoured Utility Car M20 was a variation of the M8 Greyhound, which mounted a .50in Browning HMG on a ring mount. This one belonged to Gen George S. Patton (seen at rear, leaning on the HMG) as the Third (US) Army signs denote. (Patton Museum)

Data: Personnel Carrier M3
Battle Weight: 20,000lb
  (9,090kg)
Engine: White 160AX, 147hp
Max Speed: 45mph (72kph)
Radius of Action: about 200 miles
  (320km)
Length: 20ft 3in (6.17m)
Width: 7ft 3.5in (2.2m)
Height: 7ft 5in (2.25m)

Recce Vehicles

The USA produced four-, six- and eight-wheeled armoured cars, four- and six-wheeled scout cars during World War II. The main types are listed in the table below:

Designation	Date into Service	No of Wheels	Main Armaments	Remarks
T25E1 and E2	1942/43	4	MG	Both were modifications of the T25 Smart scout car of 1941 with armoured bodies
T24	1942	6	MG	Willys 6 x 6 chassis no turret
T17E1 and E2 Staghound	1942/43	4	37mm on E1, twin .50 MG on E2	Not used in US Army; over 2,400 built and all sold to British
T17 Deerhound	1942	6	37mm	Welded hull and T7 lt tk turret, bow and coax MG
T22E1 and E2 Greyhound M8	1943	6	37mm	The M8 was the best US lt armd car
T26 utility car M20	1943	6	.50cal on ring mount	M8 chassis
T28 Wolfhound M38	1944	6	37mm, coax and AA MG	
T13	1942	8	37mm	Welded armour
T18E2 Boarhound	1942	8	57mm	Built for British but never saw action

Tanks

US tank policy favoured lighter tanks to those of their enemies and consequently the Sherman was outmatched by the German Tiger and Panther from the summer of 1943 to the spring of 1945. This stemmed largely from the different concepts of armoured warfare, but also because of the radical difference in getting to the battlefield. The American tanks had to be shipped for thousands of miles, land on hostile shores, in many cases amphibiously. They then had to cross innumerable rivers on temporary bridges because the original ones would be destroyed. Thus their tanks could not be too heavy. US tankers also favoured a policy of using armour for deep, long range thrusts into

An M8 Greyhound, the standard US Army armoured car, passes a German StuG 40, somewhere in Europe. The Greyhound was armed with a 37mm gun and a coaxially mounted .30in Browning MG, in a manually-operated turret. (via Tank Museum)

A Tank Recovery Vehicle (TRV) M32, based on the Sherman medium tank, with the gun turret replaced with a fixed turret fitted with a 60,000lb winch and pivoting 'A' frame jib. There was a similar TRV based on the M3 medium tank, known as the M31. (Author's collection)

the enemy's rear where they could chew up his supply installations and communications. Thus, great endurance and mechanical reliability were given priority above armoured protection and, to some extent, firepower. However, tank versus tank battles were found to be unavoidable and it was therefore decided to put a heavy tank (the M26 Pershing) into production.

GIs watching a demonstration of an M3–4–3 bow-mounted flamethrower, which had a range of 60yd and was fitted in place of the bow machine gun. (via Tank Museum)

'Aunt Jemima', the Mine Exploder T1E3(M1), was one of a range of mine-clearing devices based on the Sherman medium tank. The massive rollers exploded mines through pressure.

Tanks

Designation and Name	Weight	Crew	Armament	Length (L), Height (H) and Width (W)
M1 and M2 combat car	8.77 ton (8,945kg)	4	1 X .50cal MG 1 X .30cal MG	L 13ft 7in (4.08m) H 7ft 9in (2.33m) W 7ft 10in (2.35m)
M2 series 1t tank (weight dependent on mark)	8.4–10.3 ton (8,658–10,506kg)	4	1 X .50 and 1 X 30 MG (M2A4 had a 37mm) (M2A3 and M2A4 were both longer and taller)	L 13ft 7in (4.075m) H 7ft 4in (2.2m) W 8ft 1in (2.43m)
M3 series 1t tank General Stuart (weight dependent on mark)	12.23–14.18 ton (12,474–14,363kg)	4	1 X 37mm 3 X .30 MG (M3A3 was longer, wider and not so tall)	L 14ft 11in (4.47m) H 8ft 3in (2.48m) W 7ft 4in (2.2m)
M5 series 1t tank General Stuart (weight dependent on mark)	14.73–15.13 ton 15,025–15,402kg)	4	1 X 37mm 2 X .30 MG plus AA MG	L 14ft 3in (4.28m) H 7ft 6.5in (2.26m) W 7ft 4.5in (2.2m)
M22 1t tank (airborne) Locust	7.32 ton (7,466kg)	3	1 X 37mm 1 X .30 MG	L 12ft 11in (2.88m) H 6ft 1in (1.82m) W 7ft 1in (2.13m)
M24 1t tank Chaffee	18 ton (18,360kg)	5	1 X 75mm 2 X .30 MG plus AA MG	L 18ft (5.4m) H 8ft 1.5in (2.45m) W 9ft 8in (2.6m)
M3 series med tank Lee and Grant	26.8 ton (27,336kg)	6	1 X 75mm 1 X 37mm 3/4 X .30 MG	L 18ft 6in (5.55m) H 10ft 3in (2.98m) W 8ft 11in (2.68m)
M4 series med tank Sherman (weight dependent on mark)	29.68–32.5 ton (30,274–33,150kg)	5	1 X 75/76mm 2 X .30 MG plus AA MG	L 19ft 4in (5.8m) H 9ft (2.7m) W 8ft 7in (2.58m)
M26 hy tank Pershing	41 ton (41,820kg)	5	1 X 90mm 2 X .30 MG plus AA MG	L 28ft 10in (8.65m) H 9ft 1in (2.73m) W 11ft 6in (3.45m)

Tank Destroyers

Designation	Weight	Crew	Armament	Length (L), Height (H) and Weight (W)
Gun motor carriage M18 Hellcat	17.86 ton (18,217kg)	5	1 X 76mm 1 X .50 AA MG	L 21ft 10in (6.55m) H 8ft 5in (2.53m) W 9ft 9in (2.93m)
GMC M10 Wolverine	29.47 ton (30,059kg)	5	1 X 3in 1 X .50 AA MG	L 19ft 7in (5.88m) H 8ft 1.5in (5.47m) W 10ft (3m)
GMC M36	27.7 ton (28,254kg)	5	1 X 90mm 1 X .50 AA MG	L 20ft 2in (6.05m) H 8ft 11in (2.68m) W 10ft (3m)

A Sherman fitted with the 'Culin' hedgerow cutter for dealing with the thick bocage hedgerows in Normandy. Sgt G. Culin, the inventor, was decorated for his bright idea!

Combat cars on parade. The Cavalry had to call their tanks 'combat cars' so as not to contravene the 1920 National Defense Act which said that only the infantry could have tanks! Here LTC Ernie Harmon (later to become an outstanding division commander) leads his battalion of MIs. They were armed with both .30in and .50in machine guns in the same turret, while the tanks had two turrets side by side. (via Tank Museum)

This Rocket Launcher T34 mounted on a Sherman comprised banks of 4.5in rockets in tubes (60 in all) above the turret and was known as 'Calliope'. Note all the added sandbags to provide the Sherman with better protection. (via Tank Museum)

An early model M3A1 light tank, shortly after the battle of the Tenaru River in the Solomons. The Honey, as this little light tank was called by the British, who received large numbers of them in the Western Desert, was reliable, easy to drive and maintain, but was only armed with a 37mm gun.

End of the light tank line was the excellent M24, Chaffee, which mounted a very useful 76mm gun. This Chaffee has been painted with whitewash as ad hoc snow camouflage.

This M3 medium, Gen Lee tank and its crew were photographed 'at ease' in North Africa. The Lee was issued to US forces, while the Grant which had turret modifications (e.g. no raised comd's station) came into British service.

Fresh off the factory assembly line are four of the new medium Sherman tanks which replaced the M3 mediums. These are all the M4A1 model with a cast one-piece hull and cast turret and were probably made by the Lima Locomotive Works.

A T26E3 heavy Pershing tank, seen with its crew, soon after it had knocked out a Tiger 1 and two PzKpfw IVs. Armed with a 90mm, Pershing was the best US tank of World War II, but was not issued in any great numbers until after the war ended. (Sgt N. Mashlonik)

An M18 Hellcat tank destroyer in action during street fighting. It was light and fast, mounted a useful 76mm gun, but lacked armour protection.

An M10 Wolverine tank destroyer belonging to 701 TD Bn advances in Italy past a partially-completed Bailey bridge and a knocked-out Sherman. The British fitted the Wolverine with a 17pdr gun and called it the M10 Achilles.

The early 37mm anti-tank gun which was later replaced by the 57mm. It was also used in the Pacific for infantry support firing HE and canister. Its armour penetration was only 2.1in at 1,000yd. (via Tank Museum)

ARTILLERY

Anti-Tank Artillery

The US Army started the war with the obsolescent 37mm anti-tank gun, which was based upon the German 37mm PAK. It was, however, used for most of the war in the Pacific theatre, while elsewhere it was replaced by the 57mm (based on the British 6pdr). Late in 1942, a 'home-grown' anti-tank gun was designed, the 3in M5, which saw service both towed and as the main armament for the M10 tank destroyer.

Gun	Weight in action	Weight of shell	Maximum range	Armour penetration (at 20°)
37mm M3A1	912lb (410.4kg)	1.921lb (0.86kg)	12,850yd (11,750m)	2.1in (5.25cm) at 1,000yd (900m)
57mm M1	2,700lb (1,215kg)	6.28lb (2.83kg)	10,260yd (9,380m)	2.7in (6,75cm) at 1,000yd (900m)
3in M5	5,850lb (2,632.5kg)	15.43lb (6.94kg)	16,100yd (14,720m)	3.85in (9.63cm) at 1,000yd (900m)

Field Artillery

The production of field artillery in World War II was centred upon the 105mm howitzer which had been designed prewar, but not put into production until 1940, consequently there was none of the 'making do' with obsolete equipment that had dogged the US field artillery in World War I. Although the term 'medium artillery' was not one which the US artillery often used I have used it in this book to cover the medium calibres of 4.5in and 155mm. Heavy artillery really started with the 155mm gun (the 155mm howitzer being medium artillery) and went up to the 240mm howitzer. There were larger calibre guns, both fixed and railway mounted, used by the coast artillery, some of which I have shown at the end of the table.

Gun	Weight in Action	Weight of Shell	Max Range	Type
75mm how M1A1	2,160lb (980.6kg)	14.6lb (6.63kg)	9,760yd (8,930m)	light/pack
105mm how M2A1	4,260lb (1,934kg)	33lb (14.98kg)	12,500yd (11,438m)	field
4.5in gun M1	12,455lb (5,654kg)	54.9lb (24.9kg)	25,715yd (23,529m)	medium
155mm how M1918	8,184lb (3,715kg)	95lb (43.1kg)	12,300yd (11,250m)	medium
15mm how M1 and M1A1	11,966lb (5,432kg)	95lb (43.1kg)	16,000yd (14,640m)	medium
155mm gun M1917 and 1918M1	25,550lb (11,600kg)	94.7lb (43kg)	20,100yd (18,390m)	heavy
8in how M1	29,700lb (13,470kg)	200lb (90.8kg)	18,510yd (16,937m)	heavy
8in gun M1	69,300lb (31,462kg)	240lb (108.86kg)	35,000yd (32,025m)	heavy
240mm how M1	64,700lb (29,345kg)	360lb (163.3kg)	25,168yd (23,000m)	heavy
14in gun M1920	631,000lb (286,580kg)	1,200lb (544.3kg)	48,220yd (44,092m)	coast

Self-Propelled Artillery

America probably produced more different SP artillery guns than anyone else during World War II, the earliest being the GMC M3 which was a 75mm mounted on a halftrack. A number of 75mm howitzers were fitted to the M5 light tank chassis and formed the basis of an assault platoon and/or combat team. Though not a specific fit in TOE, many divisions, especially armoured, used these called Howitzer Motor Carriage M8. The standard 105mm howitzer was mounted on the M3 tank chassis (called the Priest by the British) and was so successful that it was decided to do the same with both medium and heavy guns. The 155mm M1918 gun was the first; mounted in a chassis derived from the M3 tank, it was called the GMC M12 and its simple layout was so successful that it has been generally followed for all subsequent SPs. The gun was mounted on a pedestal, at the rear of the chassis with plenty of space around it. There was little if any armour protection (sides only) and a rear 'spade' (cf. a bulldozer blade) was fitted which could be dug in to help counter the shock of firing. Later models included the M40, which was a newly

Replacing the 37mm was the 57mm M1 anti-tank gun which could penetrate 2.7in of armour at 1,000yd. This one was being towed into the fortress city of Metz, which Third Army eventually captured after a long siege. (Patton Museum)

The 3in anti-tank gun was the largest US anti-tank gun and was widely used and very popular. Belonging to the 90th Inf Div, this gun is on a hillside near the Saar River which is obscured by smoke, probably laid by the CWS 4.2in mortars.

One of the early field pieces was the World War I vintage M1897A2 75mm gun. Some saw service in the Philippines, but most were relegated to the training role after 1941. (via Tank Museum)

Backbone of the US field artillery was the 105mm M2A1 howitzer, this one belonging to C Bty, 10th FA of the 3rd Inf Div. Over 8,500 were produced during the war. (via Real War Photos)

Another World War I veteran was the 155mm Howitzer M1918, mounted on the M1918A3 carriage, with pneumatic tyres. Used in Italy and the Pacific as well as in the USA. (via Tank Museum)

The 155mm howitzer M1 and M1A1 was a highly successful, accurate weapon, 4,000 of which were issued. The A1 version was made of a stronger grade of steel. This 155mm belonged to the 985th FA Bn and is being fired on the Roer River front during the battle of the Hurtgen Forest in February 1945. (via Real War Photos)

A 155mm gun M1918A1 is prepared for action in the UK, October 1942. Widely used despite its age, it could fire its 95lb projectile over 20,000yd.

8in Gun M1 was a 31ton heavy gun, used for long-range bombardment. It was 10.4m long and fired a shell weighing 240lb. There were 139 built by the end of the war. As can be seen, it was towed by an M35 prime mover, which was basically an M10A1 tank destroyer minus its turret. (via Tank Museum)

75mm pack howitzer M1A1. Men of the 10th Mtn Div give a 75mm pack howitzer a final OK in the Pisa area of Italy, 26 January 1945. It is mounted on the M8 rubber-tyred carriage. Accurate, but the shell was too small to be really effective. (via Real War Photos)

T27 multiple rocket launchers could be mounted on a variety of vehicles, both lorries and tanks. Here the T27 (which held eight 4.5in rockets) is mounted in two banks on the back of GMC 2½ ton cargo trucks. The launchers could be elevated from –5° to +45°.

The Howitzer Motor Carriage M8 was based on the M5 light tank and mounted a 75mm howitzer in an open-topped turret. Nearly 1,800 were built and widely used. These M8s belonged to the First (US) Army and are in action during the Battle of Hurtgen Forest. (via Real War Photos)

The Howitzer Motor Carriage M7 was based on the M3 medium tank and mounted a 105mm howitzer in an open-topped turret. Known as the Priest by the British, the HMC M7 and M7A1 were standard equipment for all artillery battalions in US armoured divisions.

The Gun Motor Carriage M12 mounted a 155mm gun on the M3 medium tank chassis. It was used for heavy bombardment. The M30 cargo carrier was identical but minus the gun and the recoil spade.

SP guns were also mounted on halftracks, like this 75mm GMC M3, coming ashore from an LCT at Cape Gloucester in New Britain Island, South Pacific. (via Tank Museum)

The M2 .50 Browning Machine Gun was also used in the AA role as seen here, manned by men of the 1st Inf Div on training in the USA. The .30in M1917 machine gun was used also in an AA role. (via Real War Photos)

designed 155mm gun on the M4 tank chassis. This was followed by the mounting of the 8in howitzer on the same chassis (known as the M43) and finally, both the 8in gun and the 240mm howitzer were mounted on the Pershing heavy tank chassis, and known as the T93 and T92 respectively.

Anti-Aircraft Artillery

The USA produced a wide variety of anti-aircraft artillery, ranging from multiple mounted heavy machine guns up to 120mm guns. They also produced thousands of 'American Bofors' having recognised the excellence of this most successful of all light AA weapons.

There were also 105mm and 120mm AA guns produced in small numbers, but only a few of the latter ever went overseas as they were mainly used for home defence.

Gun	Wt in Action	Wt of Shell	Effective Ceiling	Cyclic Rate of fire (in rpm)
Multiple .50cal 4 X M2 MGs)	2,396lb (1,087kg)	–	low flying ac only	2,300
37mm M1	6,124lb (2,780kg)	1.34lb (.6kg)	10,500ft (3,200m)	120
40mm Bofors	55,491lb (2,517kg)	2lb (.9kg)	11,000ft (3,353m)	120
3in M3	16,800lb (7,627kg)	12.8lb (5.8kg)	27,900ft (8,504m)	25
90mm M1	19,000lb (8,626kg)	23.4lb (10.6kg)	33,800ft (10,300m)	15
90mm M2	32,300lb (14,650kg)	23.4lb (10.6kg)	33,800ft (10,300m)	27

The four heavy machine guns of a Multiple .50in Machine Gun Carriage M51, could produce a highly effective curtain of fire against low-flying aircraft. This one is covering Ludendorf Railway bridge over the Rhine at Remagen newly captured by 9th Armd Div. The M51 belonged to 639th AAA Bn, First (US) Army, March 1945. (via Real War Photos)

The Multiple GMC M15A1 comprised a 37mm M1A2 gun and two .50in MG mounted on an M3 halftrack. Manually-operated with all round traverse it could be elevated to 85˚.

The best light AA gun World War II was the Bofors 40mm which replaced the 37mm. This gun originated in Sweden of course, but was manufactured under licence in the USA and known as the 40mm gun M1. The photograph shows a Bofors set up for action in front of the Opera House in Frankfurt, 27 March 1945. (via Real War Photos)

The 3in AA Gun M3 was of World War I vintage, however, many had been modified and improved. The M2A2 mount was known as the 'spider' because of its long outrigger arms. By 1941, most were used for home defence although some saw action in the Philippines. (via Tank Museum)

The most successful and widely used heavy AA gun was the 90mm; seen here is the M1 version. The M1A1 was similar, but had the Spring Rammer M8 fitted. Both had outriggers (not fitted here because of the gunpit), but they could be folded for transportation. Note also the two large roadwheels of the AA Mount M1A1

AA guns in action. After the rangefinder and director station have located the target, the eight-man crew gets to work. Part of the crew aims in accordance with the electrically-transmitted instructions, while the ammo carriers and loader go into action. This photo shows the start of loading drill, the ammo relayer (at rear) had just passed the shell to the second relayer (hand on shell) who has inserted it into the fuse setter and struck the trip lever with his left hand.

VEHICLES

The following photographs are but a small sample of the wide range of vehicles produced by the American motor industry which included nearly 1,000,000 light trucks, 500,000 1½ ton trucks, over 800,000 2½ ton trucks and more than 150,000 trucks over 2½ tons. The various types of vehicle included the following:

Ambulances:

Truck ½ ton 4 X 4 Dodge and truck ¼ ton Jeep ambulance.

Patrol, Staff Cars and Utilities:

Car light sedan Ford; car heavy utility Ford; truck ¼ ton Jeep (many different forms); truck ¾ ton 4 X 4 command car and command recce car Dodge; truck ¾ ton 4 X 4 weapons carrier Dodge; bus 2½ ton 4 X 2 International K7.

Transport Vehicles:

Truck 2½ ton 6 X 4 cargo Studebaker ditto GMC; ditto 6 X 6; ditto cargo dump; truck 2½ ton 6 X 6 gasoline Studebaker; truck 4–5 ton 4 X 4 Federal with 10 ton refrigerated trailer; truck 4 ton 6 X 6 Diamond T; truck 4 ton 6 X 6 dumper Diamond T; truck 7½ ton 6 X 6 prime mover.

Motorcycles. MP units were one of the most prolific group users of motor-cycles. Over 60,000 Harley Davidson Model WLA were built and found in all theatres. Note the windscreen, siren and rifle bucket.

Staff Cars. There were four basic types: 5 and 7 passenger sedans and 5 and 7 passenger station wagons, the smaller being made mainly by Chevrolet, Ford and Plymouth, the larger including Buicks, Oldsmobiles, Packards and Cadillacs. (via Tank Museum)

The Jeep. Over 630,000 Jeeps were built during World War II and were used all over the world. Its robust chassis, excellent 4 X 4 cross-country performance and great adaptability made it a winner. Note the trailer, also the angle-iron on the front bumper to cut cables (which might otherwise decapitate the driver) and the .30in Browning MG. (via Tank Museum)

This home-made armoured Jeep was designed by 82nd Airborne Division and carries a .50 Browning, radio, and a mascot named 'Dutchy'! (via Tank Museum)

The 'Jimmy'. The GMC 2I/2 ton 6 X 6 truck was known as the 'Deuce and a half' or more affectionately as 'Jimmy'. A vast number of these ubiquitous load carriers were built – over 562,000 by GMC alone and 250,000+ by other manufacturers. They were also fitted with a wide variety of other bodies – tankers, operating theatres, dump trucks, mobile workshops, etc., etc. This 'Jimmy' is visiting the storm-twisted Mulberry Harbour off Omaha Beach.

Truck 41/2 ton 4 X 4 Federal with 10 ton refrigerated trailer. In this class, commercial types such as this one were purchased. Semi-trailers included gasoline tanker, box van and refrigerator van. (via Tank Museum)

A 12 ton M26 truck tractor. This 12 tonner became the standard heavy recovery vehicle, when used together with the M15 or M15A1 transporter semi-trailer. Note the armoured cab and .50cal AA MG. It was powered with a 240bhp engine and had three winches (one front and two rear). Transporters had a 40–45 ton capacity so would find no problem lifting this 30 ton Sherman. (via Tank Museum)

A WC54 Dodge 4 X 4 ambulance. between 1942 and 1944 26,000 were built. Each could accommodate four stretchers or seven sitting patients. (via Tank Museum)

A Diamond 'T' recovery vehicle just entering an Ordnance Repair centre on the ABC convoy route near Antwerp. The Diamond 'T' had twin cable-operated booms each with a 5 ton capacity that could be used together (as here) or one on either side. (via Tank Museum)

The International 4 X 2 tractor, known as the M425 and M426 by the army, was one of the mainstays of the 'Red Ball Express', with its 10 ton trailer as seen here. These four were photographed in Brest on the first anniversary of the town's liberation. (via Tank Museum)

A Truck amphibious 2½ ton 6 X 6 DUKW, which was based on the 'Jimmy' with a propeller and rudder added. On land it used its normal drive. Over 21,000 were built. This one has just landed near Toulon on the southern coast of France, 15 August 1944. (D = 1942, U = amphibian, K = all-wheel drive, W = dual rear axles.) Max load was 2.25 tons.

Two Landing Vehicle Tracked (LVT) amphibians, known as the Buffalo in UK parlance, can be seen here on the edge of the surf in this busy beach scene from Peleliu Island in the Pacific, September 1944. It lacked a hinged ramp, which was rectified with the LVT 2. Both were cargo carriers. There were also LVT (A), which were, in effect, amphibious tanks. (via Tank Museum)

The M29 Weasel was a little 2 ton tracked cargo carrier, ideal for use in snow because of its wide, rubber tracks. Here a ski patrol of the 10th Mtn Div have loaded their packs into the Weasel and grabbed the tow rope, Spigyana, Italy, 21 January 1945.

Searching for mines using the SCR 625 mine detector, in the war-torn streets of Monghiforo, south of Bologna, Italy. The SCR 625 weighed 6½lb so the operator tired quickly as he had to sweep in an arc. It would detect metal at about a foot deep, but was no use with non-metallic mines.

Another method used for mine detection was to prod with a bayonet or the special wire prodder shown here. The mine had then to be carefully dug up and defused.

Paddling stormboats across the Maas River, while larger boats await their turn, during a preliminary amphibious assault exercise in preparation for the Rhine crossing.

Engineers drive a small tracked bulldozer through Pietravairano, Italy.

An engineer using a Hough loader. This type of lightweight engineer equipment was extremely useful for the myriad small tasks which had to be tackled by the engineers. (via Tank Museum)

This pontoon bridge was constructed by the 1st Inf Div engineers, near Torcross, Devon, during manoeuvres prior to D-Day, 4 May 1944. (via 1st Inf Div Museum)

A Model C666 mobile crane on a heavy pontoon raft. This type mounted the Quick-Way crane. On the shortest 10ft radius it could lift 13,000lb, while on a 25ft radius it could lift 5,500lb. (via Tank Museum)

Some bridging projects were small, others in the mountains of Italy were somewhat larger!

An SCR536 portable 'handie-talkie' radio, the smallest Signal Corps set. The little GI was an Italian orphan, who 'attached' himself to this unit.

An SCR 300 infantry manportable radio set up here in a command post near the Ndemfoor airstrip on Hawaii. Note that some GIs wear camouflaged suits and have camouflaged equipment. (via Tank Museum)

A mortar officer uses a field telephone to send back a mortar fire plot in Lunéville, France.

A radio operator in an artillery OP near Barenton, France, sends information back to the guns. Note also the shine on the observers'
steel helmets, even through the net. Cut camouflage or hessian strip was also needed; the operator has a little, the observers none!

Amphibious Vehicles

Nowhere was amphibious warfare perfected so well as in the Pacific theatre, where, based upon the lessons learned from the landings in North Africa and Europe, the USA made a major contribution to the art of warfare. Special vessels were designed for the purpose which had the common characteristic of being equipped with a bow which could be opened to allow exit by troops, AFVs and vehicles, directly on to the beaches under their own power. Of the dozen or so types the most important were the LST (landing ship tank), LSM (landing ship medium) and the LSD (landing ship dock). Among the landing craft were the LCT (landing craft tank), the LCI (landing craft infantry) which could carry 200 men or 75 tons of cargo, the LCM (landing craft mechanised) and the LCVP (landing craft vehicle personnel) which could carry 36 men, plus one ¾ ton truck or 4 tons of cargo. In addition there were amphibious vehicles which could be launched from the ships and proceed across water and up on to the beaches under their own power. A small selection of these important amphibians is shown.

ENGINEERS

The Corps of Engineers used a wide variety of specialised equipment to assist them in carrying out their multitudinous tasks and the photographs which follow merely show some of this equipment and some of the tasks. To give some idea of the vast spread of equipment, here are but a few of the items used by the engineers:

Construction Machinery:

Augers, air compressors, cranes and shovels (tractor operated, crawler mounted and rubber tyred); crushing and screening plant; bituminous material distributors and other road making equipment; road graders; road rollers, concrete mixers; rooters, saws; (all types); scrapers (motorised, towed and semitrailers); crawler tractors; trailers (8, 16 and 20 ton) and electric welders.

Boats:

Assault M2, rubber, recce pneumatic canvas, storm (plywood), 18ft gasoline powered utility and outboard motor boats (22hp and 50–55hp).

Bridges:

Fixed Steel Bailey type M2; Box girder H-10 and H-20; 25 ton steel pontoon; M-2 treadway (including floats); M-3 pneumatic float.

Mapping Equipment:

Alidades, cameras, compasses, levels, stereoscopes.

SIGNALS

Details of the full range of US Army radio sets (short, medium and long range) are given in Appendix Seven at the end of the book. Some of the sets are pictured, also wire communications equipment. Types of the latter were as follows:

Types of Wire	Description	Talking Range
Assault Wire	very light, twisted pair which could be quickly laid over the ground. Two types: W130, wt: 30lb/mile and WD-1/TT, wt: 48lb/mile	5 and 14 miles respectively
Field wire	heavier and stronger for use in long lines on the ground or on poles. 130lb/mile W-110-B, wt:and W-143	12–20 miles and 27 miles respectively

C H A P T E R   1 0

TACTICS

Infantry/tank cooperation. The cornerstone of US Army tactics was the all arms team, with infantry and tanks working closely together, supported by the rest of the arms and services. Here tanks, loaded with infantry, belonging to the Seventh (US) Army wait for orders in the main street of Munich, 29 April 1945.

With a tactical doctrine based largely upon outdated weapons and concepts, the American Army was perhaps more profoundly impressed by the success of the German blitzkrieg of 1940 than they should have been. As we have already seen, this led to an immediate call for 50 to 60 armoured divisions and the formation of the 'Armored Force'. For a time the exponents of separate all conquering armoured forces held the stage. However, until the enemy main positions could be breached, the idea of armour sweeping into the heart of enemy territory was clearly a non-starter. The 'armour above all' lobby had as one of its major opponents

the Chief of Staff of the Army Ground Forces, Lesley J. McNair, who firmly believed that armour on its own could only be successfully used for exploitation, after more conventionally balanced forces had done the job of fixing the enemy, manoeuvring to strike them in the flank or the rear, while maintaining a reserve to exploit any advantage gained, or, if things went wrong, to cover a withdrawal. These tasks called for the traditional infantry and artillery team, but now well supported by tanks and close support aircraft. McNair was also vigorously against all types of specialised units designed to carry out only one particular type of mission. Instead, he preached flexibility and the need for the balanced team of all arms. This doctrine became the basis of American tactics once they got into their stride and it was used to great effect. However, to be fair to the exponents of the swift armoured thrust, such as Gen George S. Patton Jr, tying tanks down to a more slow moving type of battle did lead to some great 'lost opportunities'. The actual detailed use of the doctrine of course varied with the terrain and the enemy opposition. For example, in the bocage country of Normandy, the thick hedgerows and sunken roads required very close cooperation and detailed planning between armour, infantry and engineers. In the jungles of the SW Pacific, the coral atolls of the Central Pacific, the deserts of North Africa and the mountains of Italy, it was necessary to develop means of applying the doctrine to suit local conditions. However, it was clear in all cases that modern warfare required closer than ever cooperation by all arms.

ASSAULT DOCTRINE

Basic infantry assault doctrine was initially based on the covering fire tactics as used in the final phase of World War I. Each 12-man rifle squad was divided into a squad leader, a two-man scout section, a four-man fire section and a five-man manoeuvre and assault section. The scouts, with the squad leader, would locate the enemy, the squad leader would then call the fire section (which contained the BAR) to give covering fire while the third section advanced. Unfortunately, this brought only a part of the squad's firepower to bear on the enemy during the advance, and only too often the squad leader was unable to play an active part as he was pinned down with the scouts. Controlling and directing the fire of both the squad and the platoon was one of the most difficult tasks. When a platoon was engaged in a firefight it was virtually impossible for the platoon leader to control personally the fire of his complete platoon, so he had to rely on his squad leaders. In rugged terrain it was often impossible for the squad leader to direct the fire of his complete squad. In addition, all too often both the squad and platoon leader joined in the firefight instead of trying to control the fire.

So the infantry squad turned for help to the tanks and partly for this reason it became the 'norm' to assign tanks to all sizeable infantry formations. A favourite method of attack was by using an infantry company supported by a team of 3–7 tanks. Sometimes the tanks would advance first, sometimes with the infantry skirmish line, sometimes they carried the infantry on the tanks. The tanks took on the enemy

Behind the leading troops was a massive 'tail', bringing up the ammunition, gasoline and supplies which the fighting troops needed. However, this 'tail' was highly mechanised, as is evidenced from this busy scene in the Normandy beach-head area. (via Tank Museum)

strongpoints, while the infantry dealt with anti-tank weapons. Communications between all parts of the all arms force were clearly essential and success or failure could well depend upon them.

MARCHING FIRE OFFENSIVE

This type of advance was much favoured by Gen Patton's Third Army and was very successful, although it did at times result in heavier casualties. All the infantry moved forward together in a thick skirmish line, with close tank support. All the BARs and LMGs went with them and *everyone* fired at all possible enemy strongpoints which were in range, while all the large weapons that could be mustered laid down covering fire. The principles of mutual support and shock action were used to the full. Even in Italy, there were occasions when marching fire was used, although the mountainous terrain did not lend itself to this type of manoeuvre. When attacking down ridge lines, over reasonably open terrain, or on hills easily accessible to infantry, it was very effective and resulted in fewer casualties from enemy small arms fire.

USE OF ARMOURED DIVISIONS

In one of his 'Letters of Instruction' to all corps and division commanders, Gen Patton covered this important subject in some detail. In brief, the points he made were as follows: after beginning by explaining the important differences between haste and speed, he emphasised the need for armoured attacks to be as closely coordinated as in the infantry division, with the tanks, infantry and artillery all working as a team. The latter should when possible be under divisional control, with their forward observers in tanks ready to deal quickly with enemy anti-tank guns (by

It was the average GI in the infantry who did the low level fighting and thus met friend and foe alike on his two feet. Here infantrymen, carrying their two best friends – the rifle and the shovel – are embraced by welcoming French girls in a small village, July 1944.

HE, smoke or white phosphorus), enemy OPs and hostile artillery. Circumstances would dictate whether the attack would be led by tanks or by the infantry, the latter definitely leading when the attack was against known enemy anti-tank guns, extensive tank minefields, or when it was necessary to force a river crossing or a defile. When the tanks led, then they must use their guns for 'reconnaissance by fire', that is to say, shooting at likely hiding places for enemy anti-tank guns, etc. When they approached hedgerows they should comb them with machine gun fire. He goes on to recommend the use of smoke to blind the enemy OPs and guns when it was necessary to cross open ground; to deprecate the use of tanks to provide indirect fire except in an emergency and to advise against tanks entering villages (but to go in from the rear when it was really necessary). After giving some detailed points for both tank crews and armoured infantry he summarises this particular instruction thus:

> We must take great and calculated risks in the use of armor, but we must not dive off the deep end without first determining whether the swimming pool is full of water. You must never halt because some other unit is stuck. If you push on, you will release the pressure on the adjacent unit and it will accompany you. Troops are never defeated by casualties but by lack of resolution – of guts. Battles are won by a few brave men who refuse to fear and who push on. It should be our ambition to be members of this heroic group. More casualties occur

A two-man foxhole, with overhead cover, is home for two weary GIs, sleeping head to toe. Note the grenades, belts, packs, etc. outside the trench and the cut natural camouflage.

among those who halt or go to the rear than among those who advance and advance firing. Finally, all of us must have a desperate desire and determination to close with the enemy and destroy him. *

COMBAT ORDERS

Combat orders were those pertaining to operations in the field. The other general class of orders was *Routine* which included general orders, court martial orders, special orders, bulletins, circulars and memoranda.

Preparation of Combat Orders

The solution of any problem demanding action by a unit required that certain definite steps be taken by the commander in a logical sequence. First he had to make an appreciation of the situation (known as an 'estimate of the situation' in the US Army) as explained below. As a final step in this appreciation he arrived at a decision as to the action to be taken to deal with the situation. Next he made his plan to put his decision into effect, and then by means of orders, he conveyed his instructions to his subordinates who executed the operation. Finally, he had to supervise

* Extracted from: Letter of Instruction No 3 dated 20 May 1944 and issued by HQ Third United States Army.

the operation so that it was carried out as per his orders. The extent to which the commander performed each of these steps (less of course the decision which he alone could make) depended upon such factors as the size of the command, staff, state of training, etc. In the same way the task of preparing orders could vary widely according to the situation. Days or weeks might be devoted to them by the commander and his staff; on the other hand, instant action might be called for and orders could be given out over the radio when necessary.

Estimate of the Situation

This was the process of reasoning by which the commander arrived at his plan. Written estimates were practicable and appropriate at times, staff estimates were usually presented orally in brief form (either individually or in conference). The commander analysed, with respect to his mission, the terrain, dispositions of friendly and hostile troops, relative strengths of his own unit and the enemy, assistance he could expect from other troops, etc.

Close, immediate support was provided by the organic weapons in the infantry battalion, such as the 60mm mortar. This one, belonging to Co 'B', 1st Bn 60th Inf Regt, opens up from a position on the edge of Drelborn, Germany, 3 February 1945. (via Real War Photos)

He then determined the plans open to him to accomplish his mission and what the enemy could do to prevent this happening. Then, by opposing each plan by each of the enemy capabilities, he worked out which plan was most likely to succeed. The process ended with the commander expressing concisely exactly what he intended to do. He was then in a position to work out his plan.

Orders

Combat orders consisted of field orders, administrative orders and letters of instruction. Both field and administrative orders had standard sequences in order to make them easier to understand and to ensure that no vital points were missed out. Details of these sequences are contained in Appendix Five at the end of the book.

VEHICLE MARKINGS AND CAMOUFLAGE

THE UNIT CODE SYSTEM

With nearly 2½ million trucks of all types and about 90,000 tanks, not to mention 50,000 halftracks and multitudinous other vehicles, the American Army had to have a simple, straightforward way of being able to identify any vehicle and to know at a glance its parent unit. A code system was therefore introduced which could be quickly interpreted by everyone from private soldier to general officer. It was *not* meant as a means of deceiving the enemy, although it was clearly not as obvious as the use of colourful regimental crests or divisional signs which it largely replaced. On many occasions the markings used in the unit code system were deliberately concealed in battle areas. The code consisted basically of four groups of letters and numbers which were: Army, Corps and Division codes; Regimental or Battalion codes; Company codes; and finally, Vehicle numbering codes.

Army, Corps and Division Codes

This consisted of first the number of the Army concerned (in Arabic numerals) followed immediately by the letter A for Army. Next came the Corps number (in Roman numerals), followed by the letters AB or Δ if it was an airborne or armoured corps. When applicable, the Brigade number was added (in Arabic numerals), with the letters BG immediately after it. This also applied to Group numbers which were followed by GP. There were other letter codes used at a higher level, e.g. SMC Army Supply and Maintenance Command; RTC Replacement Training Centre (normally preceded by the branch symbol – see below); AADC Army Air Defence Command.

Regimental or Battalion Codes

These followed a similar pattern, i.e. the number of the regiment, battalion or detached company (in Arabic numerals) followed by the appropriate branch or service symbol. These symbols were:

AB Airborne; AA Anti-Aircraft; APH Amphibious; Δ Armored; C Chemical; E Engineers; F Field Artillery; I Infantry; M Medical; P Military Police; O Ordnance; Q Quartermaster; S Signals; TD Tank Destroyer; T Transportation.

The I and O symbols were always preceded by a dash in order to prevent confusion with numbers. Battle groups, tank battalions, field artillery battalions and reconnaissance squadrons operating under the regimental system were identified by B, Δ, F and R respectively, preceded of course by their number and followed by the basic identification of the unit concerned. The letter X was used when a unit had no intermediate organisation (e.g. at HQ level). For example: 3A—X HQ—40 = 3rd Army HQ, 40th vehicle.

Company Codes

These once more followed a similar pattern but used the company, troop or battery letter, or HQ for headquarters (and the HQ unit) and SV for service units. Independent companies also included a code which identified their role, viz:

AM ammunition; AW automatic weapons; CON construction; DP depot; DS direct support; GAM general automotive maintenance; GS general support; HW heavy weapons; MR mortar; MT maintenance; PM parachute maintenance; R reconnaissance; RP repair; TMP transportation motor pool.

Units not covered by these codes were allowed to invent their own, provided they were appropriate and did not exceed three letters.

Vehicle Numbering Code

Finally, each vehicle was given a number in sequence in the order in which they would normally appear in the unit order of march. Towed trailers were considered as vehicles and given the number directly after the towing vehicle. It followed, therefore, that numbers 1 to 10 were usually allocated to HQ vehicles in a company; 11 to 20 to the 1st Platoon, 21 to 30 to the 2nd Platoon and so on. A21 would therefore be the first vehicle of 2nd Platoon of 'A' Company.

Examples of how the code worked

1A—2Δ—67Δ—D5 = 1st Army, 2nd Armored Division, 67 Armored Regiment, 5th vehicle of 'D' Company.

V—602TD—B—9 = 5th Corps, 602 Tank Destroyer Battalion, 'B' Company, 9th vehicle.

17AB—320F—B—6 = 17th Airborne Division, 320th Field Artillery Battalion, 'B' Battery, 6th vehicle.

Placing and Application of Codes

The official location was the front and rear bumper/tailboard of soft skinned vehicles and on the front glacis plate and rear wings of tanks. Where no suitable surface could be found, then the code could, at the unit commander's discretion, be applied to the sides of the vehicle. Codes were painted as large as possible – but not more than 4in tall – ideally using stencils. An inch long dash was put in to separate each of the code groups.

NATIONAL IDENTIFICATION SYMBOLS

Six different types of national identification symbols were used, all being variants of the stars and stripes of the American flag. The most well known was the white star which was used on most Allied vehicles from the D-Day landings onwards. Taken in the order in which they first appeared they were: three-colour star; two-colour star; the national flag; star and stripe; star and circle; and finally the white star. The *Three-colour star* (Fig 33) was the first to be used and was in fact in use before the war. It consisted of a white star with a circular centre in red on a blue circular background. It was not used much after 1941 on vehicles, although aircraft carried it until about 1942. The *Two-colour star* (Fig 34) appeared in North Africa towards the end of 1942 on some vehicles; it consisted of a white star on a blue (but sometimes red) circular background. The *National flag* was used on vehicles, and on uniforms, during the North African landings of 1942, mainly for political reasons as this was the first time the American Army had participated in the European/Mediterranean theatre. The *White star and stripe* (Fig 35) was

The standard identification symbol was the white star, with or without the circle. This wrecker towing a captured German tank (PzKpfw III Ausf L) also has the unit code on the front bumper.

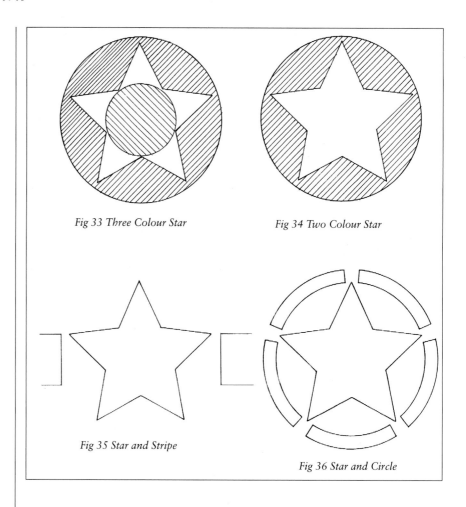

Fig 33 Three Colour Star

Fig 34 Two Colour Star

Fig 35 Star and Stripe

Fig 36 Star and Circle

used on tank turrets 1942–43. The *Star and circle* (Fig 36) again in white, comprised a star surrounded by a broken circle. It came into use during 1943 and remained for the rest of the war. It had originally been designed as a ground to air recognition symbol, but seems to have been painted on most parts of vehicles in Europe, to no set pattern. It was not as widely used in the Pacific theatre. The *White star*, a plain white star, became the most commonly used symbol, sometimes appearing with the star and circle on the same vehicles.

TACTICAL SIGNS

These signs were only used on vehicles of the combat units, so in the main they were confined to armoured fighting vehicles (AFVs), company jeeps, etc. The aim was to provide instant recognition during the heat of battle and the methods of achieving this included using names, numbers, letters and abbreviated titles. Terence Wise, in his excellent book *American Military Camouflage and Markings* also includes pin-ups and such like, 'although these were beyond the scope provided by official regulations'. He goes on to suggest that they achieved to some degree, the effect of boosting morale as well as providing identification, just as the officially discarded regimental crests had done in the past.

Tanks and other vehicles were painted a basic green and their crews would camouflage them with freshly cut natural camouflage. However, to be effective this had to be changed regularly. This Sherman was moving in a dusty part of Italy, which was a 'dead' giveaway as it was extremely difficult to conceal.

Regulations allowed major formation commanders to decide upon their own system of tactical signs, provided they kept to the following general rules:

Rule 1 Signs had to consist of geometric shapes or pattern, stripes or other simple designs, which included naming vehicles.

Rule 2 The signs had to be big enough to be read at about 100yd range.

Rule 3 They had to be as difficult as possible for the enemy to understand and not represent any unit insignia.

CAMOUFLAGE

Vehicles used three types of camouflage: natural foliage, nets and paint, or a mixture of all three. The first two do not require any further explanation as they were standard practice in any army, so we will only cover painting here. The US Army Corps of Engineers issued various standard camouflage paints in colours which included such shades as Earth Brown, Forest Green and Olive Drab. Vehicles, guns and other combat equipment were painted either all over in one colour (e.g. in temperate climates the colour was Olive Drab) or in disruptive patterns, using various appropriate colours. The main colours for the various climatic areas were as follows:

Temperate Area Olive drab, field drab (brown) or another light colour to match the particular terrain, black.

Desert Area Sand, earth yellow or red or other light colour, black.

Arctic Area White, olive drab, black.

WOMEN'S ARMY CORPS

Director of the Women's Auxiliary Army Corps, Col Oveta C. Hobby. Note the different cap badge and collar badges to those worn by the rest of the US Army officers. The collar badges feature the head of Pallas Athene, Greek goddess of war (both badges face left).

On 14 May 1942, the President signed a bill which established the Women's Auxiliary Army Corps. The basic purpose of the corps was to utilise the services of women wherever possible and thus release a corresponding number of men for combat duties. The immediate authorised strength was 25,000; however, by November 1942, the WAAC had so fully justified its purpose that the authorised strength was raised considerably and an intensive recruiting campaign started. The

first WAAC training centre was opened at Fort Des Moines, Iowa on 20 July 1942 and within four weeks a basic training course of four weeks for auxiliaries and a six weeks' course for officer candidates had been established. Later, other training centres were opened at Daytona Beach, Florida, Fort Oglethorpe, Georgia and Fort Devens, Massachusetts. The women received training in these camps to prepare them to take their place in Army life. The four weeks' basic training course was designed to inculcate the principles of army discipline, customs and courtesies as well as teaching them to look after government property! Following the basic course, WAACs might go into units or, where special talents were indicated, be sent to specialist schools for additional training. For example, they were trained as clerks, cooks and drivers. Suitable women were also given training as radio operators and radio repair, while others were trained in photographic techniques, developing and printing of pictures, camera use and repair. Potential officers received intensive training in administrative and command responsibilities. After a little more than a year, over 65,000 women had been enrolled and were serving in more than 240 posts, camps and stations in the USA and abroad. They were coping with 155 different jobs.

On 30 September 1943 the WAAC ceased to exist and the Women's Army Corps (WAC) came into existence. Their strength continued to rise until by 1945 there were nearly 100,000 WACs, including 6,000

A WAC under training learns how to fire a carbine. WACs were trained how to fire personal weapons but did not play a combat role – that has been a modern-day innovation!

WACs belonging to an all-negro postal unit sort PX items at the battalion's temporary quarters in the UK before moving to France, 13 February 1945. This unit brought the number of WACs assigned to ETO to approximately 7,500.

Good examples of different WAC uniforms: full Arctic, tropical, liner for cold weather clothing and finally, normal temperate winter uniform. (via Tank Museum)

WAACs at mess in the consolidated mess hall of the 32nd and 33rd WAAC companies, Fort Huachuca, Arizona, 9 December 1942. (WAC Museum)

Two WAAC auxiliaries servicing a truck at Fort Huachuca, 8 December 1942. I wonder how long their overalls stayed so clean! (WAC Museum)

WACs on board a troopship in the Pacific during World War II. The standee-bunks were in tiers of four in this cabin, but were probably more comfortable than naval hammocks. (WAC Museum)

WACs arriving in France disembark from an LCT at Le Havre beach in 1945. (WAC Museum)

WACs arriving by air, 'somewhere in the Pacific'. Was the pilot waving goodbye? (WAC Museum)

WACs in tropical dress, line up for chow in the Pacific theatre and are 'chatted-up' by GIs. (WAC Museum)

officers. Approximately 17,000 were on duty in overseas theatres. In addition to the jobs explained already, they also recruited and trained nearly 100 general hospital companies who assisted army doctors and nurses to care for the sick and wounded. Towards the end of the war WAC training was concentrated at Fort Des Moines, the other centres being closed down.

A survey taken in May 1943 showed that 40.9 per cent of the WACs were under the age of 25, 70 per cent were single and that the average age was 27.9. The breakdown of percentages of WACs' jobs at that time was: office and administration 64.4 per cent; technical and professional 13.6 per cent; drivers 6.6 per cent; food service 5.6 per cent; communications 2.7 per cent; mechanical, trade and manual 2.7 per cent; supply and stock 2.6 per cent and radio 1.8 per cent.

APPENDIX 1

ABBREVIATIONS

Every army uses abbreviations for words or groups of words which are in constant use, so as to save time, space, etc. However, these abbreviations must be officially authorised and not merely made up by the writer at the time, or no one will be able to understand them. The following is a list of the more common US Army abbreviations which were used in World War II, showing in three columns, the abbreviation; what it means (i.e. full American title) and the British equivalent or explanation. A blank in the final column indicates that there is no equivalent British term and where the equivalent British term is the same as the US term, the British abbreviation is given in italics.

US abbreviation	US full title	British equivalent or explanation
AA(A)	Antiaircraft (artillery)	Anti-aircraft (artillery) [*AA (Arty)*]
AA(A)IS	Antiaircraft (artillery) intelligence service	
AAF	Army air forces	
AB	Air base	Air base
AC	Air Corps	
	Accompanying artillery	Artillery in support or under command
Adrm	Airdrome	Airfield
Adv	Advance	Advance or advanced [*adv*]
Adv CP	Advance command post	Tactical HQ
A Engr Serv	Army Engineer Service	Royal Engineers
AF	Air Force	
AHQ army	Army headquarters	HQ army group or HQ army
Aid Sta	Aid station	Regimental aid post
AIS	Artillery information service	
ALP	Ambulance loading post	Casualty collecting post
Am (DP)	Ammunition (distribution point)	Ammunition (post) [*amn (AP)*]
AMecz	Antimechanized	Anti-tank
A Med Serv	Army Medical Service	Royal Army Medical Corps

187

Anl	Animal	Animal
AP	Airplane	Aircraft
App	Appendix	Appendix [*appx*]
Armd F	Armored Force	Armoured Force
Arty	Artillery	Artillery [*arty*]
AT	Antitank	Anti-tank [A tk]
Atchd (unit)	Attached unit	Unit under command
Atk	Attack	Attack
Atk ech	Attacking echelon	Leading troops in an attack
Aux arm	Auxiliary arm	Supporting arm
Avn	Aviation	
AWS	Aircraft warning service	Early warning system
Ax Sig Com	Axis of signal communication	Main signal artery
	Azimuth instrument	Theodolite
	Azimuth	Compass bearing. So 'measure an azimuth' – take a bearing
Bd	Boundary	Boundary [*bdy*]
Br	Bridge	Bridge [*br*]
BHQ	Brigade headquarters	Brigade headquarters [*bde HQ*]
	Bivouac	Harbor
Bln	Balloon	Balloon
Bn (C Tn)	Battalion (combat train)	Battalion (A echelon transport) [*bn (A ech tpt)*]
Bomb	Bombardment	
B Rcn	Battle reconnaissance	Reconnaissance [*recce*]
Brig	Brigade	Brigade [*bde*]
BRL	Battalion reserve line	Battalion reserve locality
Br Tn	Bridge train	Bridging vehicles
Btry	Battery	Battery [*bty*]
Btry Ex	Battery executive	Gun position officer
C	Combat, corps, or chief	Battle, corps, or chief
Cam (Bn) (Co)	Camouflage (battalion) (company)	Camouflage [*cam*]
	Canteen	Waterbottle
Carr	Carrier	Platoon vehicle. Nearest equivalent, 15cwt truck
	Casualty agent (chemical)	War gas
CE	Corps of Engineers	Officers of the Engineer Service
C ech	Combat echelon	Fighting group
Cem	Cemetery	Cemetery
Cen	Center	Centre
CG	Commanding General	Commander of a formation
	Check concentrations	Artillery registration

CHQ	Corps headquarters	Corps HQ
	Circle aiming	Artillery director
	Circulation map	Traffic map
Clm	Column	Column [coln]
Cml	Chemical	Chemical [chem]
CO	Commanding officer (of regts, bns, and sub-units); company or combat orders	Commanding officer [CO]; company [coy] or operation order
Coll Sta	Collecting station	Advanced dressing station
Com (O)	Communication (officer)	Signal (officer)
	Combat command	Armoured brigade group
Comdr	Commander	Commander [comd]
Com Z	Communications zone	Line(s) of communication
	Conduct of fire	Fire control
	Conference call	Multiple call on telephone
Cons	Construction	Construction [constr]
	Continuing attack	Exploitation
	Control point	Traffic post
COP	Combat outpost	Outpost
	Cossack post	Observation post or listening post by night
Co T	Company transport	Company A echelon transport [coy A ech tpt]
Co Tn	Company train	Company B echelon transport [coy B ech tpt]
CP	Command post	Tactical HQ
CR	Crossroads	Crossroads [x rds]
CW	Continuous wave	Carrier wave (wireless)
CWS	Chemical Warfare Service	
CZ	Combat zone	Forward area
	Danger space	Danger area
	Dead space	Dead ground
	Decision (in orders)	Intention
Decon	Decontamination	Decontamination [decn]
	Defensive zone or defensive area	Defended locality or area
Dep	Depot	Depot [dep]
Det	Detachment	Detachment [det]
	Development	Deployment
DHQ	Divisional headquarters	Divisional headquarters [div HQ]
	Distributing point	Ammunition point, petrol point, or supply point
Div	Division	Division [div]
Ech	Echelon	Echelon [ech]
Elm	Element	Element
Emb	Embarkation	Embarkation

	Emergency barrage	Superimposed fire
Ep	Entrucking point	Embussing point
	Estimate of the situation	Appreciation of the situation
Ex	Executive	Principal staff officer of a brigade, regiment, or battalion
Excl	Exclusive	Exclusive [*excl*]
F	Field	Field [*fd*]
FA	Field artillery	Field artillery [*fd arty*]
FDC	Fire direction center	The organisation which controls the concentrated fire of the artillery battalion
Fi	Fighter	Fighter
	Filler replacements	First line reinforcements
	Fire for adjustment	Registration for correction of fire by observation
Flt	Flight	Flight [*flt*]
FM	Field manual	Military text book or pamphlet carried in the field
FO	Field orders	Operation order
	Foxhole	Weapon slit
FR	Flash ranging	Flash spotting
	Fragmentary order	Operation instruction
F Tn	Field train	Battalion B echelon transport
Fxd fire	Fixed fire	Fire on fixed lines
G	Gun	Gun
G–NP	Chemical agent, non persistent	Non-persistent gas
G–P	Chemical agent, persistent	Persistent gas
G–PF	Gas-proof building or dugout	Gas-proof building or dugout
Gp	Group	Group [*gp*]
Gpmt	Groupment	Grouping
Gr Reg	Graves registration	Graves registration
GSC	General Staff Corps	
	H hour	Zero hour
H	Horse	Horse
HD	Harbor defense	Port defence
H-Dr	Horse drawn	Horse drawn [*HD*]
HE	High explosive	High explosive [*HE*]
Hq	Headquarters	Headquarters [*HQ*]
Hy	Heavy	Heavy [*hy*]
Hwy	Highway	Main road
	Interceptor	Interception (wireless)
IC	Information center, or inspected and condemned	Report centre, or unserviceable

	Identification	Formation sign or unit flash
	Identification panel	Ground strip
Impreg	Impregnating	Impregnating
Incl	Inclusive	Inclusive [*incl*]
Inf	Infantry	Infantry [*inf*]
Instr	Instrument	Instrument
Int	Intelligence	Intelligence [*int*]
	Interdiction fire (complete)	Concentration (of fire)
	Interdiction fire (partial)	Harassing fire
IP	Initial point	Starting point
L	Light (adjective)	Light [*lt*]
Lbr	Labor	Labour [*lab*]
LC	Line of communication	Line(s) of communication [*L of C*]
LD	Line of departure	Start line
Lgts	Lights	Lights [*lts*]
	Limiting point	Junction point
LM	Land mine	Land mine
Ln O	Liaison (officer)	Liaison (officer) [*LO*]
	Logistics	Everything relating to movement, supply and evacuation
M [*mot*]	Medium or motor	Medium [*med*]; or motor
Mat	Material	Material
Mbl	Mobile	Mobile [*mob*]
MC	Medical Corps	Officers of the Medical Services
Mecz	Mechanized	Mechanised [*mech*]
	Meeting engagement	Encounter battle
MLR	Main line of resistance	Forward defended localities
Mort	Mortar	Mortar
M & S	Maintenance and Supply	Supply and Transport
Msg (Cen)	Message (center)	Message (signal office)
Msgr	Messenger	Orderly or despatch rider
MSR	Main supply road	Main supply route
Mtr	Motor	Motor [*mot*]
Mtrcl	Motorcycle	Motorcycle [*MC*]
Mtz	Motorized	Motorised [*mot*]
Mun	Munitions	Munitions
NCS	Net control station	Control station (wireless)
Nt	Night	Night
O	Officer; order; or orders	Officer [*offr*]; order or operation order [*OO*]
Obsn	Observation	Observation
Obsr	Observer	Observer
Odly	Orderly	Batman
OP	Observation post	Observation post [*OP*]
OPL	Outpost line	Outposts

OPLR	Outpost line of resistance	Outpost line
Opn	Operation	Operation [op]
	Oral order	Verbal order
Orgn	Organization	Organisation [org]
	Parenthesis	Brackets or inverted commas
	Passage of lines	Leapfrogging
P & D Sec	Pioneer and demolition section	
Pers	Personnel	Personnel
Pion	Pioneer	Pioneer
Pk	Pack	Pack
Plat	Platoon	Platoon [pl]
Pon	Pontoon	Pontoon
	Post exchange	Canteen
	Prearranged fire	Predicted fire
Pt	Point	Point [pt]
Prcht	Parachute	Parachute [para]
	Prime mover	Towing vehicle
Pvt	Private	Private [pte]
Py	Party	Party
	Quadrant	Field clinometer
QMC	Quartermaster Corps	Supply and transport services
Qr	Quartering	Quartering
R (Co)	Rifle (company)	Rifle (company)
R (O) (P)	Regulating (officer) (point)	Regulating (point)
Rad	Radio	Wireless
	Range quadrant	Range dial
RB	Road bend	Bend in road
Rcn	Reconnaissance	Reconnaissance [recce]
Rcn (Air)	Reconnaissance (air)	Tactical or strategical reconnaissance
RCT	Regimental combat team	Infantry brigade group
Rd	Road	Road [rd]
Regt	Regiment (infantry or armored)	Regiment [regt]
Repl	Replacement	Replacement
	Requisition	Indent
Res	Reserve	Reserve [res]
	Retrograde movement	Withdrawal
Rhd	Railhead	Railhead [RH]
RHO	Railhead officer	Officer in charge of railhead
RJ	Road junction	Road junction [rd junc]
RR	Railroad	Railway [rly]
Rr Gd	Rear guard	Rearguard [reargd]
RRL	Regimental reserve line	Brigade reserve locality
RS	Road space	Road space
SA(Am)	Small arms (ammunition)	Small arms (ammunition) [SA(A)]

Sales Comm (Bn)	Sales commissary (battalion)	NAAFI
Salv	Salvage	Salvage [*sal*]
S & B	Sterilization and bath	Mobile laundry and bath unit, RAOC
Sb	Switchboard	Switchboard [*swbd*]
	Scheme of maneuver	Plan of attack
Sct	Scout	Scout
	Sector of fire	Arc of fire
	Security detachment	Protective or covering detachment
	Sentry squad	Sentry post
Sep	Separate	Separate
Serv Tn	Service train	Units of the supply service
S & F Bn	Sound and flash battalion	Survey regiment, RA
	Shelter area	Harbor or bivouac area
Sig	Signal	Signal [*sig*]
SL	Support line	Reserve locality
Slt	Searchlight	Searchlight [*SL*]
Sn	Sanitary	Sanitary
SOI	Signal operation instructions	
SOP	Standing operating procedure	Standing orders for war
SPM	Self-propelled mount	Self-propelled mounting [*SP*]
Sq	Squadron	Squadron [*sqn*]
Sq (Air)	Squadron (Air)	Squadron [*sqn*]
SR	Sound ranging	Sound ranging [*S rg*]
Stf	Staff	Staff
Strag L	Stragglers line	A line on which stragglers posts are established
Sup Pt	Supply point	Supply point [*sup P*]
Surv	Survey	Survey [*svy*]
T (Co)	Transport (company)	Transport (company) [*tpt (coy)*]
TD (Bn)	Tank destroyer (battalion)	Anti-tank regiment RA
	Telescopic panoramic	Dial sight
Tg	Telegraph	Telegraph [*tele*]
Tgp	Telegraph printer	Teleprinter
	Time interval	Time allowance
Tk	Tank	Tank [*tk*]
Tn	Train	Transport [*tpt*], sometimes train
TO	Tables of organization	War Establishments
Tp	Telephone	Telephone [*phone*]

Tr(s)	Troop(s)	Troop(s) [*tp*]
Trac	Tractor	Tractor
Traf	Traffic	Traffic
	Treadway bridge	Track bridge
Vis	Visual	Visual
	Wire line	Cable route
Wpn	Weapon	Weapon
	Wrecker	Recovery vehicle
W Sup	Water supply	Water supply
	Zone defense	Defence in depth

MILITARY SYMBOLS

USE OF COLOURS

The two basic colours were blue and red:

Blue All formations, units, installations, etc., in territory occupied by own or Allied troops.
Red All formations, units, installations, etc., in territory occupied by the enemy.

The only exceptions to this rule were that Gassed areas were always shown in Red; areas on to which Allied fire or gas was to be brought down were shown in Blue.

IDENTIFICATION OF FORMATIONS AND UNITS

Symbols to show identification of formations and units were built up by a combination of basic signs as follows:

Armies and Corps	Size Symbol	
	Army or Corps No	
Divisions, brigades, regiments and independent units or sub-units	Size Symbol	
	Type Symbol	Number of formation or unit
	Size Symbol	
Units and sub-units forming part of a formation or unit	Type Symbol	Number of formation or unit
	Weapon Symbol	

Type Symbols

Air Corps ∞

Armd ⊂⊃

Horsed Cav ⟋

Mech Cav ⊘

Horsed Mech Cav ⟋

Arty (other than coast arty) •

Coast Arty AA △

Engr E

Chem warfare G

Sig Corps S

Inf ⊠

Mot Inf ⊠ **MTZ**

Para Inf ⊠ **PRCHT**

TD TD

Med Corps ⊞

QM Corps Q

Tptn Corps ⊛

Vet Corps ⊽

Size Symbols

Sqd •

Sect • •

Pl • • •

Coy, Tp, Bty or Air Corps Flt   I

Bn, Cav Sqn or Air Corps Sqn   II

Regt or Gp   III

Bde, CC or Air Corps Wing   X

Div or Airforce   X X

Corps   X X X

Army   X X X X

Corps area, dept or sect of Com Z   o o o

Titles

Titles of armies were written in ordinal letters within the basic symbol: eg First, Second, etc. Corps titles were written in Roman figures within the basic symbol: eg I, II, IX, etc. Numbers of other formations, units and sub-units were written in Arabic figures.

Examples of Use

Second Army

1st Bn 8th Fd Arty

1st Armd Div

Mortar Sect, C Coy, 18th Inf

3rd Inf

Boundaries

Boundaries were shown by inserting in a broken line the size symbol of the formation unit, etc, to which the boundary refers: eg

Army Boundary —— X X X X ——

Regt Boundary —— III ——

Headquarters

The position of an HQ was shown by the basic symbol
The foot of the pole marks the exact location of the HQ. The nature and size of the HQ
was shown by the addition of the appropriate size and type symbols: eg

HQ 12th Corps

HQ 1st Recce Bn

HQ 1st Inf Div

Miscellaneous US Military Symbols

Boundaries

Front line

Outpost line — OPL —

Main line of resistance — MLR —

Support line — SL —

Bn reserve line — BRL —

Regt reserve line — RRL —

Straggler line — P —

Line of communications — LC —

Limiting point —⊗—

Line of departure — LD —

Line beyond which respirators — G —
must be at alert

Limit of wheeled traffic by day — DY —

Limit of wheeled traffic by night — NT —

Line beyond which lights on vehicles — LT —
are prohibited

Weapons

Arrow to point in principal direction of fire. Unless otherwise stated indicates .30cal H MG. Placed under
symbol of unit of any arm, this symbol indicates MG unit of that arm.

	In Position	Emplacement unoccupied		In Position	Emplacement unoccupied
Automatic rifle	→	---→	How or Mortar bty	●●●●	○○○○
MG	•→			▮	▯
.50cal	•⁵⁰→		or		
Lt	•L→		Cal and type shown by adding figures or description:		
AA	•AA→				
ATk (figs denote cal)	●75/AT		37mm gun	● 37mm	○ 37mm
Atk showing principal direction of fire	●75/AT→	●75/AT⤏	81mm mortar	—●81 mm	—○ 81mm
Gun	●	○			
Gun Bty	▮	▯	4.2in chem mortar	—●4.2 Cml	—○4.2 Cml
How or mortar	▬●▬	▬○▬	Barrage (in blue) Size indicates extent, notation the type	155 mm How	

Installations and Establishments

Aerodrome

   Landing Field

   Advanced Landing Field adv

Depot (supply point) ◯

Obsn post △

Searchlight

Signal

   Radio station or RS ∘

   Radar station or RC ∘

   Radio intercept station

   Wire on ground

   Sound locator

Field Defences and Obstacles

Trench (for one squad)

For each additional squad add one traverse. Proposed trenches shown in dotted lines

Dugout (isolated) ■

   In trench system

   Gas proof ■ G – PF

Entanglements

   Wire

   Concealed

Obstacles

   Individual

   Road block

   Bridge out

   Tank barrier

   Tank trap

Demolitions

   Individual — bridge,
   culvert etc, crossed out in blue

   Area covered by demolitions
   or obstacles (in blue)

Mines

   Individual ⚲

   Minefield

Gas and Smoke

Gassed area to be avoided (in red)

Area probably affected by gas
cylinder cloud

Area to be gassed, non-persistent
(in blue) (G –NP)

Area to be gassed, persistent
(in blue) (G – P)

Chem land mine

Area to be blanketed with
smoke, time effective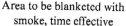

GENERAL ORDER FORM FOR A COMPLETE WRITTEN FIELD ORDER

Issuing unit
Place of issue
Date and hour of issue
FO————————————
Maps: (Those needed for an understanding of the order.)

1   Information: Include appropriate information covering:

 a   *Enemy*: Composition, disposition, location, movements, strength; identifications; capabilities. Refer to intelligence summary of report when issued.

 b   *Friendly forces*: Missions or operations, and locations of next higher and adjacent units; same for covering forces or elements of the command in contact; support to be provided by other forces.

2   Decision or Mission: Decision or mission; details of the plan applicable to the command as a whole and necessary for coordination.

TROOPS

(Composition of tactical components of the command, if appropriate.)

3   Tactical Missions for Subordinate Units: Specific tasks assigned to each element of the command charged with execution of tactical duties, which are not matters of routine or covered by standing operating procedure. A separate lettered subparagraph for each element to which instructions are given.

Instructions applicable to two or more units or elements or to the entire command, which are necessary for coordination but do not properly belong in another subparagraph.

4 Administration Matters: Instructions to tactical units concerning supply, evacuation, and traffic details which are required for the operation (unless covered by standing operating or administrative orders; in the latter case, reference will be made to the administrative order).

5 Signal Communication

a *Orders for employment* of means of signal communication not covered in standing operating procedure. Refer to signal annex or signal operation instructions, if issued.

b *Command posts and axes of signal communication:* Initial locations for unit and next subordinate units; time of opening, tentative subsequent locations when appropriate. Other places to which messages may be sent.

Commander

Authentication
Annexes (listed)
Distribution
Notes

1 Complete oral or dictated field orders follow generally this same form; fragmentary orders conform to appropriate portions.

2 The form of the order, such as special methods of indenting, lettering, and heading paragraphs and subparagraphs, is of minor importance.

3 *Heading:* The heading contains the designation of the issuing unit, place of issue, date and hour of issue, serial number of the order, and reference to the map(s) used.

Under requirements of secrecy the official designation of the issuing command may be shown by a code name and the place of issue omitted.

The date and hour are written in the sequence: day, month, year, and the hour the order is signed.

Orders are numbered consecutively for the period of the war. If two or more are issued on the same day they are given separate numbers.

The map reference designates the map(s) required, giving the scale, name of sheets, and year of edition (where necessary). The reference should include only those maps to be used in connection with the order. When the order is accompanied by an operation map, and no other map is required, the reference may be simply 'Map: Opn Map (Annex 1)'.

4 *Distribution of troops:* The distribution of troops shows the tactical groupings into which the command is divided (advance guard, main body, etc.) and the troops assigned to each. Its use generally is limited to march advance guard, rear guard and outpost orders, and to the first field order issued by a newly created command.

APPENDIX 4

COMPLETE ADMINISTRATIVE ORDER

Issuing unit
Place of issue
Date and hour of issue
ADM O——————————— To accompany FO——————————
Maps: (Those needed for an understanding of the order.)

1 Supply
    a *Rations and forage*
       1 Supply point(s) – location and units served.
       2 Time schedule of distribution (may be separate).
       3 Annex, plan of supply or rations and forage (when issued).
    b *Ammunition*
       1 Supply points – location and units served.
       2 Credits – quantities (days or units of fire) allocated to subordinate units for stated period(s). (In large units, credits in terms of types, calibres, and rounds will be allocated in the administrative order.)
       3 Dumps – limitations, if any, on stocks in dumps.

2 Evacuation
    a *Casualties*
       1 Personnel
          a Collecting station(s) – location(s) (division).
          b Clearing station(s) – location(s) (division).
          c Hospitals (station, evacuation, surgical, and convalescent) – location (army and corps).
       2 Animals
          a Collecting station(s) – location(s).
          b Veterinary evacuation hospital(s) – location(s) (army only).
    b *Burial*
       1 Instructions.

      2   Cemetery(ies) – location(s).

   c   *Salvage:* Collection and disposition – reports.

   d   *Captured material:* Disposition – reports.

   e   *Prisoners of war*

      1   Collection point(s) – location(s) (division).

      2   Inclosure(s) – location(s).

      3   Responsibility for evacuation.

3   Traffic

   a   *Circulation*

      1   Designation of main supply road(s).

      2   Assignment of routes for special purposes, when necessary.

      3   Marking of routes, when necessary.

      4   Traffic priorities, such as troop movements, class III and class V supplies, fortification materials, class I supplies, etc.

   b   *Restrictions*

      1   Limits of daylight traffic and use of lights when necessary.

      2   Movement of transportation; location(s) of forward initial point and rear initial point (where escorts are provided).

   c   *Control*

      1   Traffic control posts, when necessary – locations.

      2   Officers' control stations, when necessary – locations.

   d   *Construction and maintenance of routes*

      1   Roads – priority of work on roads and bridges; general character of maintenance; bridge loads; coordination with road work of higher and subordinate units.

      2   Railroads – same general character of instructions as for roads, including yards and sidings (army or detached corps).

4   Service Troops and Trains

Bivouacs, release, movements, special missions, attachments, etc.; when applicable.

5   Personnel

   a   *Stragglers*

      1   Straggler line – location.

      2   Collecting point(s) – location(s).

   b   *Surplus baggage*

Disposition of items such as individual packs, and extra clothing.

   c   *Mail:* Collection and distribution.

   d   *Shelter*

      1   Assignment.

      2   Quartering parties.

   e   *Strength reports*

When to be submitted and as of what date.

   f   *Replacements*

      1   Requisitions – when to be submitted.

      2   Assignment – locations, number per organisation, date and hour.

6 Miscellaneous
   a *Rear boundary* – location.
   b *Rear echelon of headquarters* – location.
   c *Protected areas (or zones in large commands)* – locations, giving boundaries.
   d *Administrative matters not otherwise covered.*

Commander

Authentication
Annexes
Distribution

Notes
1 a The form of the order, such as special methods of indenting, lettering, and heading paragraphs and subparagraphs, is of minor importance.
   b Standing operating procedure will obviate the necessity of some items.
   c Include only items which are changed.
2 Include hour and date of opening if not open already.
3 Subparagraphs similar to *b* with reference to other supplies and types within classes are added as necessary.

APPENDIX 5

NUMBER OF ENGINEERS

Numbers of engineers (units and strengths) in the Army Ground Forces (AGF), Army Service Forces (ASF) and Army Air Forces (AAF) as at 30 June 1945 (a).

Type of Unit	Number	Strength
AGF		
Divisional		
Combat bns inf div	66	42,042 (b)
Combat bns mtn div	1	807 (b)
Engr sqns cav div	1	674 (b)
Engr bns armd div	16	10,784 (b)
Engr bns airborne div	5	2,050 (b)
Total:	89	56,357
Non Divisional		
Combat bns	204	127,270
Hy pontoon bns	15	5,652
Combat coys (separate)	7	1,129
Depot coys	54	10,599
Lt equipment coys	38	4,567
Lt pontoon coys	44	9,027
Maint coys	83	15,334
Treadway bridge coys	33	4,446
Other engr ground force type	238	19,585
Total:	716	197,609
Total AGF:	805	253,966
ASF		
Port construction & repair HQ coys	12	3,026
Special bdes	3	17,927
Gen service regts	79	94,429
Special service regts	5	6,405
Construction bns	36	29,539
Gen service bns (separate)	8	5,283
Special shop bns	4	3,435

Base depot coys	24	3,786
Base equipment coys	31	5,195
Dump truck coys	135	14,200
Forestry coys	23	2,505
Hy shop coys	27	4,422
Parts supply coys	16	2,763
Petroleum distribution coys	59	12,323
Fire fighting pls	92	2,547
Utility detachments	85	3,857
Other engineer service force type	421	24,758
Total ASF:	1,060	236,400
AAF		
Engr aviation regts	11	4,568
Engr aviation bns	124	88,555
Engr aviation camouflage, topographic and utilities bn	6	2,444
Other engineer air force type	120	10,634
Total AAF:	261	106,201
Grand Total Engineers All Types:	2,126	596,567

Notes:

(a) excludes engrs with all comz and zone of interior overhead, such as European theatre HQs, service command station complement, replacement training centres and schools.

(b) strength allowed by War Dept actions as shown in 1 July 1945 WD Troop Basis.

Source: Statistics, troop units section US Army in World War II MS in OCMH.

COMPOSITION OF THE THIRD ARMY, 10 NOVEMBER 1943

(Illustrative of Army and Corps Organisation in the Army Ground Forces)

Corps in Third Army

Branch	Army Troops (Non-Corps)	IX Corps	X Corps	XVIII Corps	XIX Corps	VIII Corps
	1 Cav Div	6 Inf Divs	4 Inf Divs	2 Inf Divs	2 Inf Divs	
			1 Armd Div	1 Armd Div	2 Armd Divs	
AA	2 Brig HQ					
	4 Gp HQ					
	8 Bns					
Armd	1 Tank Gp HQ	1 Tank Gp HQ	2 Tank Bns	5 Tank Bns	2 Tank Bns	
	3 Tank Bns	1 Tank Bn				
Cav	1 Bde		1 Regt, Mech	1 Regt, Mech	1 Regt, Mech	
			1 Recce Sqn			
Chem	5 Decon Coys			2 Chem Bns		
	1 Depot Coy			Mot		
	3 Maint Coys					
Engrs	2 Combat Gp HQ	3 Combat Gp HQ	2 Combat Gp HQ	2 Combat Gp HQ	1 Top Coy Corps	
	1 Bn Sep	9 Combat Bns	6 Combat Bns	4 Combat Bns	1 Treadway Bridge Coy	
	5 Combat Bns	1 Combat Coy, Sep	1 Lt Equip Coy	2 Lt Pont Coys		
	5 Hy Pont Bns	3 Lt Equip Coys	2 Lt Pont Coys	1 Treadway Bridge Coy		
	1 Top Bn	1 Lt Pont Coy	1 Maint Coy			
	1 Water Supply Bn	2 Maint Coys Corps	1 Top Coy,			

Corps in Third Army

Branch	Army Troops (Non-Corps)	IX Corps	X Corps	XVIII Corps	XIX Corps	VIII Corps
	2 Cam Coys	1 Top Coy, Corps	1 Treadway Bridge Coy			
	1 Depot Coy					
	1 Dep Trk Coy					
	2 Lt Equip Coys					
	2 Maint Coys					
	1 Top Coy Corps					
	1 Treadway Bridge Coy					
Fd Arty	1 Gp HQ	1 HQ IX Corps Arty	1 HQ X Corps Arty	1 HQ XVIII Corps Arty	1 HQ XIX Corps Arty	1 HQ VIII Corps Arty
	2 155m How Bns	2 Gp HQ	4 Gp HQ	2 Gp HQ	4 Gp HQ	1 Obsn Bn
		1 Obsn Bn	1 Obsn Bn	1 Obsn Bn	2 155mm Gun Bns	
		4 155mm Gun Bn	4 155mm Gun Bns	2 155mm Gun Bns	4 155m How Bns	
		1 115mm How Bns	8 155mm How Bns	2 155mm How Bns		
		5 105mm How Bns	2 105mm How Bns	4 4.5in Gun Bns		
Inf		2 Inf Regts			2 Armd Inf Bns	
Med	4 Gp HQ	1 Bn HQ				
	2 Amb Bns	1 Amb Coy				
	9 Med Bns	1 Clearing Coy				
	1 Gas Treat Bn	2 Coll Coys				
	1 Amb Coy					
	13 Clearing Coys					
	26 Coll Coys					
	1 Depot Coy					
	1 Sanitary Coy					
	3 Vet Coys					
	6 Evac Hosps SM					
	2 Labs					
	2 Vet Evac Hosps					
MP	3 MP Bns			2 MP Coys		
Ord	2 Am Bns					
	1 Ord Bn					
	20 HQ Ord Bn					
	8 Am Coys					
	8 Dep Coys					
	2 Evac Coys					
	7 Hy Auto Maint Coys					
	10 Hy Maint Coys (Field Army)					
	4 Hy Maint Coys (Tank)					
	1 Lt Maint Coy					
	1 Maint Coy (AA)					
	19 Med Auto Maint Coys					
	13 Med Maint Coys					

Corps in Third Army

Army Troops Branch (Non-Corps)	IX Corps	X Corps	XVIII Corps	XIX Corps	VIII Corps
QM	1 Trk Regt				
	2 HQ Trk Regts				
	2 HQ QM Bns				
	5 HQ QM Bns (Mob)				
	4 HQ Tr Tptn Bns				
	2 Gas Supply Bns				
	1 Serv Bn				
	1 Ster Coy				
	4 Bakery Coys				
	3 Car Coys				
	4 Depot Coys				
	2 Ldry Coys				
	6 Pk Trs				
	5 Railhead Coys				
	1 Salvage Coll Coy				
	24 Troop Trans Coys				
	33 Trk Coys				
Sig	1 Armd Sig Bn	2 Sig Bns	1 Sig Bn	2 Sig Bns	
	2 Cons Bns	1 Rad Int Coy		1 Rad Int Coy	
	2 Opn Bns				
	1 Cons Coy				
	1 Dep Coy				
	2 Opn Coys				
	2 Pigeon Coys				
	1 Photo Coy				
	2 Repr Coys				
TD	1 Bde HQ	1 Gp HQ	2 Gp HQ	2 Gp HQ	1 Gp HQ
		5 TD bns	6 TD Bns	5 TD Bns	5 TD Bns
Misc	7 Bands	1 MRU (Mob)	1 MRU (Mob)		1 MRU (Mob)	1 MRU (Mob)
	14 HQ Special Troops				
	1 MRU (Fixed)				

GROUND RADIOS

Designation	Description
Short Range (up to 25 miles, but usually 5 miles or less for RT sets)	
Portable Sets	
SCR131 and 161	Two-man pack sets providing continuous wave morse signals up to five miles, on 4–5mc, prewar set still used for trg.
SCR194 and 195	One-man pack sets providing voice signals only on 27–65mc; the first Army 'walkie-talkie'.
SCR284	Both portable and vehicle borne, providing both continuous wave and voice, rather heavy (about 250lb) complete.
SCR288	A stopgap set for SCR284.
SCR300	The renowned walkie-talkie, an FM set manually tuned over 40–48mc, other versions were SCR619 for arty and the AN/GRC-12 for the armored force.
SCR509	AFII, an 80-crystal (any two frequencies preset) push-button FM radio. SCR709 version had fewer crystals, SCR609 and 809 were the field arty equivalents.
SCR511	Portable cavalry guidon set, widely used by the infantry.
SCR536	The handie-talkie, smallest Signal Corps set, a very popular AM set, with tropicalised and disguised versions.
SCR694	Both portable and vehicle borne, successor to the SCR284 to whose crystal control it added two preset frequencies. Its receiver alone was known as the SCR714. A later improved version the AN/GRC9 had a range of 75 miles.
AN/PRC3	Portable microwave transceiver developed for the field arty to replace signal lamps.
Vehicle Sets	
SCR171 and 178	Carried by vehicle, but operated on the ground with a 15-mile range on continuous wave only, 2–3mc.
SCR179 and 203	Cavalry saddle sets (SCR179 was a saddle version of the SCR178).
SCR209 and 210	Continuous wave, tone and voice sets for the Armored Force.

SCR293 and 294	The first FM sets for the Armored Force, crystal-controlled, providing voice comms only on 20–27mc.
SCR508-AFIII	An 80-crystal (any 10 frequencies preset) push-button radio-transmitter and two receivers with variations SCR528 (transmitter and one receiver) and SCR538 (one receiver) SCR708, 728 and 738 were crystal-saving versions. All provided voice only on 20–28mc, FM.
SCR510	Similar to the portable SCR509 but designed for vehicles only. SCR710 had fewer crystals.
SCR608, 628 and 610	Similar to AF sets 508, 528 and 510, but designed for the field arty with 120 crystals on 27–39mc.
SCR808, 828 and 810	Crystal-saving versions of SCR608, 628 and 610.
AN/VRC3	An FM set designed for tanks on the same frequency band as SCR300 to enable tank crews to talk to infantry using the walkie-talkie.

Medium Range (25–100 miles)
Portable Sets

SCR177	Vehicle-carried but operated on the ground, providing continuous wave, tone and voice.
SCR543 and 593	Vehicle and ground sets for the coast arty; the receiver portion SCR593 was portable.
AN/TRC2	A version of SCR694 designed for 8 to 10 pack for jungle or mountain use, providing a continuous wave range up to 100 miles.

Vehicle Sets

SCR 193	Set could be operated to provide continuous wave tone while the vehicle was moving.
SCR245	Popular mobile set providing four crystal-controlled frequencies, selected by switches.
SCR506–AFII	Standard medium range vehicle set providing on four crystal-controlled frequencies continuous wave and voice.
SCR583	A saddle or vehicle set designed to replace the short range SCR203.

There were also numerous transportable radio relay equipments, both terminal and relay sets, employing directional beams in VHF, UHF, and SHF; FM or pulse-time modulated.

Long Range (100 miles and over)
Portable Sets

AN/PRC1 and 5	Suitcase continuous wave sets designed for Military Intelligence Service (MIS).
AN/TRC10	A large but still portable set also for MIS.

Mobile Sets (operated in trucks on the move or at rest and powered by trailer-borne generators)

SCR197	Powerful set on 1–18mc with five pre-set frequencies.
SCR505 (AFI) and SCR597	Development of the former was supplanted by designs of the latter to provide 100 miles on voice, 350 miles on continuous wave (5,000 miles ground to air) having three push button channels in range 2–20mc.
SCR299	Excellent long range set mounted in a panel truck and powered by the PE95 generator carried in a two-wheeled trailer. It replaced the SCR597 and became standard for all the Army. Version SCR499 was housed in a standard shelter HO17, mountable in any 2½ ton truck. An air transportable version SCR499 became standard for the AAF. These sets radiated about 350W of power, giving a dependable 100-mile range on voice while in motion and many hundreds of miles on continuous wave in Morse code.

Transportable Sets

SCR698	Largest of SCR radio sets, a kilowatt broadcast transmitter used (together with receiver and monitor set SCR696) by MIS (Psychological Warfare Units) for broadcasting to enemy and conquered countries.

DIVISIONAL SHOULDER PATCHES

Div	Type	Nickname	Insignia	Overseas Theatres
1st	Infantry	Big Red 1	Red 1 on olive-drab shield	North Africa, Sicily and Europe
2nd	Infantry	Indianhead	Indian's head in natural colours facing left with blue warbonnet on white star in a black shield	Europe
3rd	Infantry	Marne	Alternate blue and white diagonal stripes in a square	North Africa, Sicily, Italy and Europe
4th	Infantry	Ivy	Four ivy leaves attached to a circle in a khaki diamond	Europe
5th	Infantry	Red Diamond	A red diamond	Europe
6th	Infantry	Sightseeing Sixth	A red six-pointed star	Pacific
7th	Infantry	Bayonet	Two sevens forming a black diabolo in a red circle	Pacific
8th	Infantry	Pathfinder	A yellow arrow passing through a white eight in a blue shield	Europe
9th	Infantry	The Old Reliables	A petalled flower, red on top, blue on bottom half with a white centre, all in khaki circle	North Africa, Sicily, and Europe
10th	Mountain	Mountaineers	A dark blue tab with the word Mountain worn over blue rectangle bordered by white with two red crossed swords, edged with white, in its centre	Italy
11th	Airborne	Angels	A blue shield under a blue tab with the word Airborne in white. In the centre of the shield a red circle edged with white containing number 11; two white wings sprouted at the top	Pacific
13th	Airborne	None	A yellow-winged unicorn within a blue shield topped with a blue tab bearing Airborne in yellow	Landed in France 6 Feb 45, but due to aircraft shortages did not see action

Div	Type	Nickname	Insignia	Overseas Theatres
17th	Airborne	Golden Talon	A yellow eagle's claw within a black circle edged with khaki, under a black tab bearing the yellow word Airborne	Europe
24th	Infantry	Victory	A green taro leaf edged in yellow on a red circle edged with black	Pacific
25th	Infantry	Tropical Lightning	A red taro leaf edged in yellow with a bolt of yellow lightning through its centre	Pacific
26th	Infantry	Yankee	A monogram of letters Y D in dark blue on a khaki triangle	Europe
27th	Infantry	New York	A monogram of the letters N Y in red over red stars forming the constellation Orion (after World War I commander Maj-Gen J. F. O'Ryan) within a red circle on top of a dark blue circle	Pacific
28th	Infantry	Keystone	A red keystone (unit from Pennsylvania – the Keystone State)	Europe
29th	Infantry	Blue and Grey	A Korean monad with dark blue on the left and grey on the right	Europe
30th	Infantry	Old Hickory	A red oval blue-edged, with a horizontal blue H. A Roman numeral XXX in blue within the H's bars	Europe
31st	Infantry	Dixie	A white circle edged red with two red letters D, back to back in its centre	Pacific
32nd	Infantry	Red Arrow	A red arrow pointing upwards with short red line running horizontally through its centre	Pacific
33rd	Infantry	Prairie	A dark blue circle with yellow cross in its centre	Pacific
34th	Infantry	Red Bull	A dark blue olla (a Mexican flask) with a red bull's skull in its centre	North Africa, Italy
35th	Infantry	Sante Fe	A dark blue circle with white crosses of the type used to mark the Sante Fe trail	Europe
36th	Infantry	Texas	A grey Indian arrowhead with a green capital T in its centre	Italy, Europe
37th	Infantry	Buckeye	A red circle edged in white	Pacific
38th	Infantry	Cyclone	A shield, the left half blue and the right red, with a white monogram CY in its centre	Pacific

Div	Type	Nickname	Insignia	Overseas Theatres
40th	Infantry	Sunshine	A yellow sun on a blue Diamond	Pacific
41st	Infantry	Sunset	A setting yellow sun in a half circle of red, sinking behind a line of dark blue	Pacific
42nd	Infantry	Rainbow	A rainbow from top right to bottom left, with three colours – from top: red, yellow, blue	Europe
43rd	Infantry	Winged Victory	A red clover shape with a black grape leaf in its centre	Pacific
44th	Infantry	None	A yellow circle edged blue with two blue number 4s back to back forming an arrowhead pointing upwards	Europe
45th	Infantry	Thunderbird	Originally a yellow swastika on a red diamond but changed to a yellow Indian thunderbird (unit mostly from Oklahoma) on a red diamond	Sicily, Italy, Europe
63rd	Infantry	Blood and Fire	A yellow bayonet pointed upwards with a drop of red blood on its point, on top of a red fire in the centre of a khaki teardrop	Europe
65th	Infantry	Battle Axe	A white halberd blade on a blue shield	Europe
66th	Infantry	Panther	A black panther with red tongue and white teeth within an orange circle edged in red Later design was just the panther's head	Europe
69th	Infantry	Fighting 69th	A red 6 and a blue 9 edged in white interlocked on a white square	Europe
70th	Infantry	Trailblazer	A white axehead on a red background with green trees and land with a white mountain in the background	Europe
71st	Infantry	Red Circle	The blue number 71 on a white circle edged in red white circle edged in red	Europe
75th	Infantry	None	A shield edged in khaki and divided diagonally from left to right, into red, white and blue, with a blue 7 and a red 5 in the centre	Europe
76th	Infantry	Onaway Liberty Bell	A red shield with a narrow band of blue at the top with an even narrower green band directly under that. On top of	Europe

Div	Type	Nickname	Insignia	Overseas Theatres
			the blue, a white symbol like the letter E lying on its side	
77th	Infantry	Statue of Liberty	A blue geometric shape which is wider at the bottom than at the top with a yellow Statue of Liberty at its centre	Pacific
78th	Infantry	Lightning	A red semi-circle with white lightning bolt from top right to bottom left	Europe
79th	Infantry	Cross of Lorraine	A Cross of Lorraine on a blue shield	Europe
80th	Infantry	Blue Ridge	A khaki shield edged in white with three grey mountains on a white line in the centre	Europe
81st	Infantry	Wildcats	An angry black cat, front left paw raised, facing left, in black on a khaki circle edged in black	Pacific
82nd	Airborne	All American	AA in white letters in a blue circle within a red square under a blue tab with Airborne in white letters	Sicily, Italy, Europe
83rd	Infantry	Thunderbolt	OHIO in yellow within the letter O in the centre of a black triangle – point down	Europe
84th	Infantry	Railsplitters	An all-white axe embedded in a white log inside a red circle edged in khaki	Europe
85th	Infantry	Custer	The red letters CD in a khaki circle	Italy
86th	Infantry	Black Hawk	A large spread black hawk with a red shield, with BH in black on its chest, all inside a red shield	Europe
87th	Infantry	Golden Acorn	A yellow/red acorn in a green circle	Europe
88th	Infantry	Blue Devils	Outlines of two blue number 8s, one horizontal and one vertical	Italy
89th	Infantry	Rolling W	A black W within a brown circle edged in black	Europe
90th	Infantry	Tough Ombres	A red monogram of the letters TO in a square representing the states from which the unit was recruited: Texas and Oklahoma. The nickname is a corruption of the Spanish for Tough Men	Europe
91st	Infantry	Powder River also Fir Tree	A green fir tree	Italy

Div	Type	Nickname	Insignia	Overseas Theatres
92nd	Infantry	Buffalo	A black buffalo on a tan circle edged in black	Italy
93rd	Infantry		Grey-blue French helmet on a black circle	Pacific
94th	Infantry	Neuf Quatres	A black 9 and khaki 4 in a circle diagonally divided, khaki on left and black on the right	Europe
95th	Infantry	Victory	A red 9 and a white V interlaced on a blue oval	Europe
96th	Infantry	Deadeye	A blue diamond overlapping a white diamond, the whole on a khaki hexagon	Pacific
97th	Infantry	Trident	Neptune's trident in white on a blue shield	Europe
98th	Infantry	Iroquois	An orange Indian profile, facing left, with three feathers in a blue shield edged in orange	Pacific
99th	Infantry	Checkerboard	A blue and white checkerboard in the middle of a black shield	Europe
100th	Infantry	Century	A yellow 100 in a blue shield	Europe
101st	Airborne	Screaming Eagles	A white eagle's head with black eyes, yellow beak, and red tongue, facing left in a black shield under a black flash with AIRBORNE written in yellow	Europe
102nd	Infantry	Ozark	A large yellow O surrounding a yellow U holding up a yellow Z on a blue circle	Europe
103rd	Infantry	Cactus	A green cactus growing out of a blue ground in front of a yellow sky, all in a circle	Europe
104th	Infantry	Timberwolves	A grey timberwolf head with open mouth, facing left, on a light green circle	Europe
106th	Infantry	Golden Lion	A golden lion head facing front, with features outlined in red, in a blue circle edged	Europe
	Americal	None	The white stars of the Southern Cross on a blue shield	Pacific
	Phillipine	None	Yellow head of a steer on a red shield	Pacific
1st	Cavalry	The 1st team	A large yellow shield with a black diagonal line running top left to bottom right through the centre; a black horse head in the top right-hand corner	Pacific
2nd	Cavalry	None	A large yellow shield with a blue chevron at the bottom	North Africa

Div	Type	Nickname	Insignia	Overseas Theatres
			and two blue eight-pointed stars above	
1st	Armored	Old Ironsides	The standard armoured triangle divided into three with the top yellow, bottom left blue and bottom right red. Division number in black on the yellow section. In centre an armoured vehicle track in black under a red lightning bolt	North Africa, Italy
2nd	Armored	Hell on wheels	As for the 1st	North Africa, Sicily, Europe
3rd	Armored	Spearhead	As for 1st	Europe
4th	Armored	None*	As for 1st	Europe
5th	Armored	Victory	As for 1st	Europe
6th	Armored	Super Sixth	As for 1st	Europe
7th	Armored	Lucky Seventh	As for 1st	Europe
8th	Armored	Iron Snake, Thundering Herd, Tornado	As for 1st	Europe
9th	Armored	Phantom	As for 1st	Europe
10th	Armored	Tiger	As for 1st	Europe
11th	Armored	Thunderbolt	As for 1st	Europe
12th	Armored	Hellcat	As for 1st	Europe
13th	Armored	Black Cat	As for 1st	Europe
14th	Armored	Liberator	As for 1st	Europe
16th	Armored	None	As for 1st	Europe
20th	Armored	None	As for 1st	Europe

* 4th Armoured was occasionally called 'Breakthrough' but they considered that 4th Armoured was name enough.

BIBLIOGRAPHY

Bradford, George R. *Armour Camouflage and Markings North Africa 1940–43*, Arms & Armour Press.

Chamberlain, Peter and Gander, Terry. *World War 2 Fact Files*, Macdonald and Janes.

Chamberlain, Peter and Ellis, Chris. *British and American Tanks of World War II*, Arms & Armour Press.

Crookenden, Napier, *Dropzone Normandy*, Ian Allan Ltd.

Crow, Duncan (ed.) *American AFVs of World War II*. Profile Publications.

Hofmann, George F. *The Super Sixth*, Six Armored Division Association.

Katcher, Philip. *The US Army 1941–45*, Osprey.

Rosignoli, Guido. *Army Badges and Insignia of World War 2*, Blandford Press Ltd.

Weigley, Russell F. *History of the United States Army*, BT Batsford Ltd.

Seacoast Artillery and *The Army Almanac* both published by the Military Service Publishing Company of Pennsylvania.

Stanton Shelby, L. *Order of Battle, US Army World War II*, Presidio, 1984

Publications of the US Army Center of Military History, various volumes of the following series:

United States in World War II, 'The Organisation of Ground Combat Troops'; 'The Organisation and Role of the Army Service Forces'; 'The Chemical Warfare Service: Chemicals in combat'; 'The Corps of Engineers: troops and equipment'; 'The Ordnance Department: on beachhead and battlefront'; 'The Quartermaster Corps: organisation, supply and services'; 'The Quartermaster Corps: operations in the war against Germany'; 'The Signal Corps (3 vols): the emergency, the test and the outcome'; 'The Transportation Corps: responsibilities, organisation and operations'; 'The Transportation Corps: operations overseas'; 'The Women's Army Corps'; 'The Procurement and Training of Ground Combat Troops'.

Army Historical Series, 'American Military History'; 'The Sinews of War: Army Logistics'.

US Army Lineage Series, 'Armor – Cavalry'; 'Infantry'.

Medical Department in World War II, 'Organisation and administration in World War II'.

The following Pamphlets and Reports were used:

Biennial reports of the Chief of Staff of the United States Army to the Secretary of War for the following periods: 1 July 1939 to 30 June 1940; 1 July 1941 to 30 June 1943; and 1 July 1943 to 30 June 1945.

After action report for the US Third Army
Various Tables of Organisation and Equipment (T/O & Es) as detailed in
    diagrams
Orbat of the US Army in World War 2 – European Theatre of Operations

Main War Department Field Manuals used:
FM 21–30 Conventional signs, military symbols and abbreviations
FM 5–6 Operations of Engineer Field Units
FM 7–15 Infantry Field Manual – Rifle Company, Rifle Regiment
FM 21-100 The Soldier's Handbook
Field Service Pocket Book – Part II, pamphlet No 4A staff organisation
    and staff duties in the US Army 1944

INDEX

Notes: **Bold** page references indicate illustrations.
Italic page references indicate tables.